THE CHRISTIAN COMMUNITY

Biblical Foundations

JESÚS A. DIEZ CANSECO

WESTBOW
PRESS®
A DIVISION OF THOMAS NELSON
& ZONDERVAN

WestBow Press books may be ordered through booksellers or by contacting:

WestBow Press
A Division of Thomas Nelson & Zondervan
1663 Liberty Drive
Bloomington, IN 47403
www.westbowpress.com
844-714-3454

ISBN: 978-1-6642-7630-7 (sc)
ISBN: 978-1-6642-7631-4 (e)

Print information available on the last page.

WestBow Press rev. date: 08/24/2022

DEDICATION

TO PEOPLE OF GOOD WILL

TABLE OF CONTENTS

PREFACE

This book speaks of the Christian Community as an integral part the human community. Communitarian life implies that men relate to one another in a unifying and edifying manner by virtue of sharing in the same human nature, which is innate to all of them. The Christian community, in specific terms, is a way of life whereby men, in addition to relating to one another, also relate to Christ, the God incarnate, the Son of Man.

In its religious dimension, the Christian community transcends the limitations of a historic entity, and, in its earthly dimension, is subject to the historic and evolutionary laws proper to the human race.

In its first chapters, this book describes the original human community as a form of live where men live in equality and harmony. What equality are we talking about? The equality existing in men as a result of possessing the same human nature. Therefore, it goes without saying that such equality does not refer to the individual attributes, which make each person unique within the human collectivity. These attributes, when used properly, have the potential of contributing to and solidifying human unity.

What harmony we are talking about? The harmony which generates peaceful coexistence among men, and, systematically, eradicates destructive conflicts. This peaceful coexistence does not necessarily imply absence of conflicts but rather the capacity of men to resolve them before causing mutual destruction. Communitarian life is, precisely, the fertile field for resolving conflicts.

The reader will find frequent references to the differences between men's life in *common unity* (or communitarian life) and men's life in a class society, with the latter being the most prevalent in the world since men divided themselves in antagonistic classes.

The biblical quotations contained in this book are taken from "The New American Bible – Revised Edition". The criterion for the selection of the biblical texts is based on their relevance to the human community, in general, and to the Christian community, in particular.

The purpose of the book is to offer readers an opportunity to understand the society in which they live, to allow them to gain awareness of the existence of societal conflicts, and to assist them in taking an active role in the resolution of said conflicts following the model and example revealed by Christ Jesus.

The author.

Chapter I

MAN IS A COMMUNITARIAN BEING

$\mathcal{S}$ince the beginning of its evolution, the human race presents itself as an elemental community: the community of a man and a woman, which ensures the procreation of the human species. *"It is not good for the man to be alone"* (*Genesis* 2:18). The unity between a man and a woman gives continuity to humankind. *"Be fertile and multiply; fill the earth and subdue it"* (*Genesis* 1:28).

The Book of Genesis describes the first form of communitarian life as a *"garden in Eden"* (*Genesis* 1:28). The Greek term "Eden" means "earthly paradise", and highlights a state of unity and harmony in the relations between human beings as well as between them and their Creator.

When men live in community, they assume the collective task of being agents of dominion over nature. This task is fulfilled, not by isolated individuals but by everybody acting together as a collective entity. It is not possible for man to live alone because he cannot evolve in isolation from the rest of his fellow human beings. Thus, the communitarian man settled *"in the garden of Eden, to cultivate and care for it"* (*Genesis* 2:15). It was a world characterized by harmony between man's work and nature's productivity, by harmony between producers and consumers, harmony between planning and execution. It was a form of life, which set the tone for the continuity and progress of the human race on earth.

This original state of human life is also known as The Primitive Human Community, the only form of life, which could ensure the evolution and the survival of humankind. It was a way of life where men worked in cooperation with one another as much as it was necessary and beneficial for everybody. No biological species can appear or continue to exist on earth, unless its members have the capacity to multiply, to protect and to organize themselves in accordance with an established and appropriate order.

The biblical concept of the first human community puts emphasis on the harmonic relationships among the first humans, as well as on the existence of an order established by the Creator and manifested in the communitarian behavior of men. This behavior encompassed all aspects of collective life in that men's actions were relevant to the community, and the individual tasks found their purpose in the collective benefit they generated. The communitarian order, based on common property, was the result of the rational and deliberated decision of the members of the Primitive Human Community.

This collective accord acted as a barrier to prevent individuals from appropriating for themselves the goods belonging to the community because when every person has what he needs, it is absurd to take more than what is needed. This was the form of collective life, which through hundreds of thousands of years, cemented in man his communitarian character.

The image of the communitarian man is the image of God. *"Let us make human beings in our image, after our likeness"* (*Genesis* 1:26). God speaks of himself in the plural for he himself is a community: the Trinity, a community encompassing the Father, the Son, and the Holy Spirit; three distinct and individual persons who, by virtue of the love they have for one another, constitute one indivisible God. On the other hand, human beings project the image and likeness of their Creator whenever they live in a community in which they care for the wellbeing of everybody, without exception. The image of God, therefore, is revealed when individual human beings converge in *common unity.*

1. How does God live in the trinitarian community

- God the Father lives as *"a merciful and gracious God, slow to anger and rich in kindness and fidelity"* (*Exodus* 34:6). God the Father demonstrates that he *"so loved the world that he gave his only Son, so that everyone who believes in him might not perish but might have eternal life"* (*John* 3:16). This is the way the Father lives: He gives all he is and all he has for the welfare of humanity.
- God the Son, the fullness of life in freedom, takes on the life of a man so, by his obedience, the world may be redeemed. By doing the works of his Father, God the Son fully reveals his Father. This is how he does so: by forgiving his enemies, by doing good to those who do wrong to him, by blessing those who curse him, by freeing the prisoners, and by healing the sick. God the Son lives a life of self-sacrificing love (the only true love) so we may live.
- God the Holy Spirit is incessantly encouraging us to do the works of the Father, as the Son shows them to us. So that, by doing them, we may be united in the life of the Triune God.

The life of the Triune God is the model for all human life and, when we follow such model, we become inserted in the Trinity, in God himself. The following is one example of how we can live the life of the Trinity: *"Brothers . . . mend your ways, encourage one another, agree with one another, live in peace, and the God of love and peace will be with you"* (*2 Corinthians* 13:11).

The Trinity is the perfect model of open interaction: the interaction of three Persons who have nothing to hide from each other, who are true to one another, who live for one another. This is the model of interaction the members of the human community ought to follow.

As members of this collectivity, we are called to be part of the Trinity: baptize them *"in the name of the Father and the Son, and of the Holy Spirit"* (*Matthew* 28:19), which is an invitation for us to live as the Father, the Son and the Holy Spirit live; retaining our individuality while sharing in one indivisible nature with all other human beings.

The Trinity lives in those who do not hide anything from others, in those who promote peace, unity, and equality, for they are witnesses of God's unity before the eyes of humanity.

The communitarian God continues to speak to us through his Holy Spirit, the Spirit of truth, who *"will guide [us] to all truth"* (*John* 16:13). This truth is in the Father, was revealed by Jesus, and is explained to us by the Spirit of God who lives in us. In the Christian Creed we say we believe in "the true God" in order to emphasize that the trinitarian God is true, that his communitarian life is true, that Christians must emulate communitarian life for it is true life.

2. The breakup of the unity in the Primitive Human Community

The biblical narrative concerning the breakup of the unity among the inhabitants of the *Garden of Eden* corresponds to the historical event, which caused the end of unity among the members of the Primitive Human Community. The first is the religious version, the second is the historic version. The historic break involves a process whereby small groups of people, moved by the greed to accumulate wealth, appropriated for themselves the material goods belonging to the entire community. This is how it occurred: when material possessions were held in common, and when needs were appropriately met, there came individuals who, out of selfish convenience, proceeded to enrich themselves. This was done through obtaining an excess of economic goods, and, at the same time, taking dominion over the victims of dispossession. This economic usurpation engenders a state of conflict between the perpetrators and their victims. The perpetrators become rich, and the victims, poor. It is the time in history when the powerful and the weak appear, when social antagonisms confront man against man, and when class struggle becomes the norm.

From the ashes of the Primitive Human Community emerges a societal order characterized by conflict, legalized by the law, and intent of perpetuating the existence of the powerful and the weak, the rich and the poor, rulers and subjects. Man had destroyed the community... and *"the Lord God therefore banished him from the garden of Eden"* (*Genesis* 3:23).

Chapter II

THE CALL TO RESTORE THE HUMAN COMMUNITY

*C*onsidering that the existence of antagonistic socioeconomic classes is an anomalous state of human life, it becomes imperative to restore the communitarian way of life. The efforts to achieve this goal, however, are confronted with obstacles such as the apathy of people who appear to be submerged in the dehumanizing sleep of indifference; the inertia of others who are carried away by the splendor of the irrelevant and the routine of nothingness, dazzled by the excesses of materialistic living, trapped in the exploitation of man by man, and the destruction of one another. *"They will not know [the consequences] until the flood comes and carries them all away"* (*Matthew* 24:39).

We all have the responsibility to join efforts in order to restore unity in the world. Nevertheless, some will do it, and others will not, depending on whether we are capable or not of understanding that God himself leads a communitarian life, and that he wants to share his life with us.

So interested is God in our unity that he comes to the world to help us in the task of restoring communitarian life. Yes, Jesus has come to us, but we are asleep. Wake up! *"It is the hour now for you to awake from sleep"* (*Romans* 13:11) and see the world in which we live. To be awake means to be able to remove the layers of darkness and indifference that prevent us from seeing the conflicts and destruction prevalent in our world.

What do we need to remove?

- We need to remove the false values and ideals from our hearts and minds that make us believe peace is achieved through war, that the common good is achieved through the accumulation of wealth in the hands of few, and that the life of a person is enhanced by the death of another.
- We must remove obstacles such as our own self-interests, self-centeredness, and laziness that prevent us from advocating for unity and equality among men.
- We must *"throw off the works of darkness [and] put on the armor of light"* (*Romans* 13:12).

In order to restore unity and peace in the world, nations *"shall beat their swords into plowshares and their spears into pruning hooks; one nation shall not raise the sword against another, nor shall they train for war again* (*Isaiah* 2:4).

1. Understanding the reasons why we must restore the human community

The more we understand the reasons why we must strive for the restoration of the human community, the more efficacious our efforts will be. In a world where people show little understanding of what the human community is, it is logical that they may also show little interest in promoting its restoration.

Why does the world show little interest in promoting the restoration of the human community in accordance with the model of the trinitarian community? Because the world promotes its own gods. Namely, the god of wealth and dominion, the god of war and destruction, the god of selfishness and indifference. Those who follow the world's mentality are fully convinced that there is nothing better than the gods they already possessed. They are firm believers that the Redeemer of mankind is nothing but an intruder. A spoiler, who comes to disrupt the existing "order".

However, the God incarnate, Jesus, wants us to know his coming is inevitable. He wants us to know he is the true savior, the one who has the power to free us from the divisions among us, from the devastation caused by fratricidal conflicts. If we do not want to miss his coming, we must be *awake.*

Who is awake?

He who is awake works for and looks forward to bringing unity and equality to humankind. He who is awake wants to meet God and cherish the life of unity he stands for. He who is awake will eagerly wait for the coming of the communitarian God.

When we remain awake, we live as a visible testimony to the presence of God in the world. Therefore, we can say that we already have the life of God in our midst. *"You were enriched in every way with all discourse and all knowledge, . . . so that you are not lacking in any spiritual gift"* as you strive for the coming of God (*1 Corinthians* 1:5-7).

When the world needs God, God makes himself man

One of the principal tenets of Christianity is that Christ comes to the world as the Second Person of the Trinity in order to restore in men God's communitarian way of life. And why is this so? Because the world needs it! Because nowadays many nations are *"in dismay, perplexed"* (*Luke* 21:25), suffering from economic inequalities, torn by dissent, destroyed by wars, afflicted by hunger and disease, oppressed by powerful groups, and submerged in chaos.

We live in a world that has become *"drowsy from carousing and drunkenness and the anxieties of daily life"* (*Luke* 21:34). A world that is drowsy from the abuse of power. A world that distorts the truth in order to justify a state of division and antagonisms. It exists to perpetuate the exploitation of man by man while, at the same time, creating uncertainty and aimlessness.

When people accept to receive the communitarian God and commit themselves to eradicate injustice, they are acknowledging that their *"redemption is at hand"* (*Luke* 21:28), and that *"the Lord [is] our justice"* (*Jeremiah* 33:16), so that we may make his justice a reality in our world. With the coming of Christ to our world, we must make ourselves worthy of standing in his presence by changing division into unity, war into peace, conflict into negotiation, death into life, enmity into friendship, destruction into reconciliation, and indifference into action.

2. The need for individual and collective transformations

The restoration of the human community requires a process of profound transformations both at the individual and the collective levels. This process consists of the followings three steps:

A. Acknowledgment of the presence of evil

The process begins when men acknowledge *"their sins"* (*Matthew* 3:6). This is when they see the existence of conflicts and antagonisms in themselves and in the world. Those, who are not sincere in acknowledging them, are thus confronted: *"You brood of vipers! Who warned you to flee from the coming wrath?"* (*Matthew* 3:7). They pretend to be righteous when, in actuality, they are responsible for the state of inequality and division in the world.

B. Conversion

Conversion is the wholehearted determination that moves a person to radically transforms his life by eradicating evil and embracing goodness; by discarding injustice and promoting justice; by detesting oppression and fostering liberation; by creating unity where there was division. Once conversion is achieved, the road is open to restore human *common unity*: *"Repent for the kingdom of heaven is at hand"* (*Matthew* 3:2).

C. Good fruits

The good fruits of conversion are unity, peace, and equality among all peoples. Those fruits are the *"evidence of your repentance"* (*Matthew* 3:8). But if there are no good fruits, there will be no true change, no true conversion. It follows, then, that the fruits of conversion must be manifested in the collective of men. That is, in the institutions of society.

Where will the transformations lead us?

They will lead us to a world of harmony and unity among all; a world where *"the wolf shall be a guest of the lamb, and the leopard shall lie down with the kid; the calf and the young lion shall browse together, with a little child to guide them . . . There shall be no harm or ruin on all my holy mountain"* (*Isaiah* 11:6, 9).

Man is not alone in his efforts to achieve needed transformations because *"the God of endurance and encouragement grants you to think in harmony with one another, in keeping with Christ Jesus, that with one accord you may glorify God"* (*Romans* 15:5, 7).

Now, our efforts must focus on the following tasks:

– The acknowledgement of anything that prevents us from fulfilling the goodness of our human nature.
– The determination to bring to an end our wrongdoings.
– The willingness to become servants of one another.

This process of transformation can be defined as *"a baptism of repentance for the forgiveness of sins"* (*Mark* 1:4), baptism which we, individually and collectively, must undertake in order to *"prepare the way of the Lord, make straight his paths"* (*Mark* 1:3), in order to invite God to walk with us on the road to reach unity and harmony among men.

There are, however obstacles along this path:

– The belief that human nature is intrinsically evil, thus, there is no goodness in it.
– The refusal to bring an end to evil deeds.
– The presence of relations based of domination, not service.

Under the circumstances indicated, it is difficult to set any positive transformation in motion. In the meantime, God remains waiting for us to start the process of eradicating the conflicts afflicting us and working towards restoring peace and harmony, with the understanding that achieving those goals can be compared to the work of *filling in every valley, making low every mountain and hill; leveling the rugged land, smoothing the rough country (Isaiah 40:4).*

The process of human transformation benefits us all

By carrying out this process of transformation, we will be *"hastening the coming of the day of God"*; we will be hastening the realization of the *"new heavens and new earth" where we will "be found without spot or blemish before [the Lord], at peace" (2 Peter* 3:12-14).

3. Why is the restoration of the human community necessary?

Because human unity is being destroyed by the injustices among men. The gospel of Luke, using a symbolic language, describes the magnitude of those injustices as *"twisted path, deep valleys, insurmountable mountains, and rough ways (Luke* 3:4-5). In our world, this language can be translated as:

- Abysmal differences between the rich (getting richer) and the poor (getting poorer).
- The existence of scandalous luxuries while many are deprived of the basic means for human subsistence.
- The control of political power by a minority while the vast majorities lack the opportunities for effective participation in their own governing institutions.
- The exclusive access to the benefits of modern technology by privileged minorities while vast majorities lack access to it.

Similarly, Luke speaks of *"winding, twisted roads"*, which can be understood as twisted ideologies leading peoples in misguided directions, promoting the exploitation of man by man, creating confusion, and degrading human dignity.

The logical question is now, how to restore the human community?
Let us present the following answers:

- By denouncing the evils of the world. That is, by unmasking the true nature and dimensions of *the deep valleys, and the twisted roads.*
- By announcing that God *"brings us joy by the light of his glory, with his mercy and justice for company"* (*Baruch* 5:9).
- By giving testimony, through personal example, of simplicity, moderation, and care for all.
- By entering into a partnership with God, a partnership established between God and us under the following terms:

  A. God commits himself *to begin and continue his work in us* (*Philippians* 1:6) until he becomes all in all.
  B. We commit ourselves to lead the world along the path of true human unity, *leveling the valleys and peaks, and straightening the twisted roads.*

The community is the environment where human dignity is realized

Unity, peace and harmony are the elements that make life worth living it. When we are confronted with the need to find out whether our life is worthwhile, there is no recourse more reliable than Christ to find the answer. We may, therefore, ask him the following question: *"Are you the one who is to come, or should we look for another?"* (*Matthew* 11:3). When God is with us, we then know our life is worth living, and therefore, worth protecting it.

This is how Christ describes a life worth living for: *"The blind regain their sight, the lame walk, lepers are cleansed, the deaf hear, the dead are raised, and the poor have the good news proclaimed to them"* (*Matthew* 11:5). In the human community, its members have the certainty and the reassurance of what a true life is. A true life becomes a reality when the life of God merges with the life of man in the world.

The world, however, lacks true life; it shows little evidence of God's life. Therefore, he comes to the world, precisely because there is little to no evidence of his life in us. He comes so that his justice may flourish in a world of injustice, so that fulfillment may bloom in the land of the barren, and peace may bring joy to all who are in mourning.

The coming of Jesus Christ is the answer to the quest for certainty demanded by people of good will. When God makes himself man in Jesus, he becomes the visible gift of liberation for mankind.

4. The peoples of the world need to know God's life

The knowledge of God's life is what makes us capable of committing ourselves to making his presence real in the world. For it is God himself who works in and through us every time we bring justice and peace to the world. God is with us so that we may *"strengthen the hands that are feeble, make firm the knees that are weak, say to those whose hearts are frightened: Be strong, fear not! Here is your God . . . he comes to save you"* (*Isaiah* 35:3-4).

The knowledge of God's life leads us to the understanding that we, humans, truly are communitarian beings, nothing less and nothing more. It is a sign of personal credibility to say who we really are. Thus, we must avoid the temptation of presenting ourselves as something we are not. As human beings, we ought to recognize that we are *a testimony to the light, but not the light* (*John* 1:8), until we become fully inserted in the light, the light of the trinitarian God, whose communitarian life irradiates upon humanity. In other words, we became bearers of the light of God whenever we allow the Second Person of the Trinity to dwell in us.

The light only shines through those who are truthful to themselves and faithful to others. Consequently, we will be able to share in the greatness of God only when we honestly say who we are. On the contrary, those who are intent on destroying the community, hide their identity and resort to lie in order to cover up their divisive deeds and present themselves as being what they are not. They engender a world of hypocrisy, where the evildoers claim to be righteous, where those who lie about themselves and claim to be good, destroy the truth and lack all moral authority to speak the truth.

When someone lacks the courage to say who he really is, fools himself, and creates chaos and confusion among those who surround him. He refuses to recognize the light, the light that reveals what is true and what is not.

"What then should we do"? (*Luke* 3:10)

In order to live in a community of peace and harmony, it is necessary to ask the following question, *"What should we do?"* The answer requires, first, an understanding of another question: *"Who are we?"* We, human beings, are the only ones who can effect a total transformation of the present world; we are the only ones who are capable of eradicating antagonisms and, rationally, promote a community of peace and harmony. That is expected of us, that is the call of our human responsibility. We cannot live in a world where we destroy one another; we cannot live in a world we cannot change.

The question, *"What should we do?"* relates to how we conduct ourselves in order to be what we are. The answer to this question is two-fold:

A. The answer to humanity in general (that is, to all without exception) is: *"Whoever has two cloaks should share with the person who has none. And whoever has food should do likewise"* (*Luke* 3:11). In other words, all the resources of the world belong to all of us by virtue of our human equality.

B. The answer to specific groups (that is, to all the groups with specific roles in society) is that each and every one of us must fulfill his or her role in accordance with our human dignity.

God can help us find the answers to our questions

The time is here for us to *"make [our] request known to God"* (*Philippians* 4:6). Yes, the Almighty has already heard our questions about *"who we are"* and *"what we should do"*. And his answer is that our human dignity is so great that he himself saw it appropriate to become a man, and he invites us to join him. This is who we are and this is what we should do.

5. The birth of Jesus and the restoration of the human community

Christ Jesus – God made man – comes to the world in order to restore the life of the communitarian God among men, that is, in order to invite them to return to the trinitarian God. Christ comes to a world where fratricidal conflicts are threatening to destroy it. He comes to a world in which man is no longer the highest dignity in creation; a world in which men fail to respect the dignity of one another; a world in which men treat one another as if they did not share the same dignity.

Every person coming into the world brings the image and likeness of God. But class societies try to suppress that image and likeness in us either before birth, at birth, or after birth (just like Jesus himself suffered mistreatment from a very early age).

Jesus' birth is be beginning of a process of transformation of a world of darkness into a world of light, into a world which hears the voice of God: *"Do not be afraid; for behold, I proclaim to you good news of great joy that will be for all people . . . a savior has been born for you who is Messiah and Lord"* (*Luke* 2:10-11).

What is the world of light?

It is a communitarian world wherein men treat one another as the image of God; a world into which God comes in order to merge his life with man's; a world which reflects the unity of heaven and earth. A world which can proclaim: *"Glory to God in the highest and on earth peace to those on whom his favor rests"* (*Luke* 2:14). A communitarian world is *"vast and forever peaceful,"* a world the Almighty *"confirms and sustains by judgment and justice, both now and forever"* (*Isaiah* 9:6).

When God becomes man, he restores the image and likeness of God in us; he brings an end to the world of divisions and antagonisms. With his birth, Christ *"brings glad tidings, announcing peace, bearing good news, announcing salvation"* (*Isaiah* 52:7). He also brings the means to attain what he announces: He bears *"his holy arm in the sight of all the nations"* (*Isaiah* 52:10).

Christmas is a time of liberation for a world subjected to fratricidal conflicts, it is a time when Christ begins to restore the universal brotherhood among men. The liberation, however, is ignored by those who fail to accept the restoration of the human community: *"He came to what was his own, but his own people did not accept him"* (*John* 1:11). Those who do not accept God have already accepted something else – they have accepted their worldly idols.

Christmas is the restoration of the order that has existed since the beginning of the world. *"In the beginning . . . all things came to be through him, and without him nothing came to be. What came to be through him was life, and this life was the light of the human race"* (*John* 1:1-4).

The birth of Christ will continue to be a revelation of the liberating presence of God. Christmas will continue to be God's tireless efforts to restore the original goodness inherent to human nature since its inception. This is why we celebrate Christmas every year.

Those who receive God, *"become children of God"* (*John* 1:12), God's *"holy arm in the sight of all nations"* (*Isaiah* 52:10), and God's heralds of the communitarian life in the world.

From the time of his coming into the world, the God Incarnate is confronted by a society which is ruled by powerful economic, political and military entities. The gospel of Luke describes how the Roman Empire rules unimpeded upon their subjects; entire families are uprooted and moved to distant places in order to record their existence. The sufferings of Mary and Joseph along the trip from Nazareth to Bethlehem, their inability to find shelter, and the manger that serves as a crib for the newborn Jesus are some of the injustices inflicted by a world in which even new comers are mistreated or, even worst, not allowed to be born at all (*Luke* 2:1-14).

The newborn savior comes to restore, in us, our dignity of being the image and likeness of God; he comes to a world intent on turning men into mere tools at the service of the governing elites; he comes to redeem a world intent on suppressing the God who dwells in us.

The savior's plan is to bring to people *"abundant joy and great rejoicing . . . For the yoke that burdened them, the pole on their shoulder, and the rod of their taskmaster [have been] smashed"* (*Isaiah* 9:2-3). This joy comes from the fruits of hard work, from the victory which crowns a hard-fought battle, from the victory of light against darkness, from the victory of unity over division, from the victory of freedom over all types of chains, in brief, from the triumph of the human community over societal fragmentation.

In the struggle for the restoration of the human community, men are not alone, they are actively involved in the execution of the plan designed by the communitarian God since the beginning of time.

Chapter III

THE HUMAN COMMUNITY
AND THE HUMAN FAMILY

Inasmuch as the human community finds its biological foundation in the family, Christ, the Second Person of the Trinity, had to come to the world as the member of a human family from which he received the sustenance and protection every human being needs. His human family protects the infant Jesus whenever his life is threatened by the powerful rulers of his time – the "organized society." Jesus' family is the only refuge God (in the form of an infant) can find in a world dominated by self-serving groups.

Just as King Herod wanted to *"search diligently for the child"* (*Matthew* 2:8) and kill him, so too, do the powerful rulers demonstrate total disregard for human life and do not hesitate to destroy it if their power is threatened. The infant Jesus personifies the dependence of a person on others. Jesus was denied protection and nurturing by the "organized institutions" of the world into which he was born. The powerful not only did not welcome him, but did try to kill him as an infant. Mary and Joseph (the family of Jesus), however, made it possible for him to survive his infancy.

1. The God incarnate is born into a family and is raised as a member of a society

The family of Mary, Joseph, and Jesus sets the model of life for all human families and all human institutions. The role of the family becomes especially relevant in view of the failure of other societal institutions (political, socioeconomic, and so forth) to protect and nurture human life, and to promote unity, and mutual respect. Just as the family of Mary and Joseph cared for and protected their infant son, so must society care for and protect the life of everybody. Christ lives as a member of the family of Mary and Joseph so that all human beings may live as members of the human community... *in common unity.*

History demonstrates that the unity of the Primitive Human Community broke up when men divided themselves into antagonistic groups. Nevertheless, Mary and Joseph demonstrated they were capable of preserving the unity within the community of their family. Therefore, human relations within a society must follow the model of the relations within a family. Those who honor their mother and father also honor God (*Sirach* 3:6-7). Subsequently, those who honor any person are also honoring God, and those who mistreat mother, father, or anybody, are mistreating God.

This is the nature of the relations between men, whether in a family or in society at large: "*As God's chosen ones, holy and beloved [we must relate to one another with] heartfelt compassion, kindness, humility, gentleness and patience, bearing with one another and forgiving one another*" (*Colossians* 3:12-13)." By relating in this manner, we will be able to establish "*the bond of perfection*" (*Colossians* 3:14) among all men, we will be able to "*let the peace of Christ control [our] hearts, the peace into which [we] were also called in one body*" (*Colossians* 3:14-15), into one family, into one world, the world God considers his family.

The *bond of perfection* among the members of the human family is established by the unity in which we all are to live.

The family, as the elemental cell of the human community, made it possible for Jesus to advance in "*wisdom and age and favor before God and man*" (*Luke* 2:52). The family provides the means for men to perfect their relations between themselves and between them and God.

God comes to our world as a member of the family of Mary and Joseph so that we, all human beings, may become members of the human family.

How does God define his family?

According to Luke's gospel, when Mary and Joseph realized that their son was not with them, they immediately *began to look for him with great anxiety* (*Luke* 2:48) until they found him in the temple. It is at this time that Jesus defines his family as a two-fold entity: he belongs to the family of Mary and Joseph, and also to the family of God. Jesus says to Mary and Joseph, *"why were you looking for me? Did you not know that I must be in my Father's house?"* And he *"went down with them and came to Nazareth, and was obedient to them"* (*Luke* 2:51). In this family, *"Jesus advanced in wisdom and age and favor before God and man"* (*Luke* 2:52). It is in his human family where the God-made-flesh obtains the fullness of his humanness.

The human relations within society must follow the model of the relations within the family

Those who honor their mother and father are pleasing to God (*Sirach* 3:3). Subsequently, we may say that those who honor any other person are also pleasing to God. And just as anyone who mistreats mother or father, mistreats God, so does anyone who mistreats anybody else.

2. The role of Mary and Joseph in the family of Jesus

Mary and Joseph established their human family emulating the responsibilities of the communitarian God whose Second Person had come to the world. Those responsibilities are the following:

A. The responsibility of bringing God into the world

Just as Mary gave birth to the Son of God, so too can all human beings bring God into the world through their efforts to liberate a world trapped in fratricidal conflicts, division, and self-destruction.

B. The responsibility of naming God

Just as Mary and Joseph consented to name their Son, *"God is with us"* (Emmanuel) (*Matthew* 1: 23), so too can we all name God: "God is with us" every time we live as witnesses that *God is in our human nature.* Conversely, he who does not show with his life that God is in his human nature cannot give God the name: God is with us.

Furthermore, by acknowledging that the *name* of each person is *God is in our human nature*, we are acknowledging that the greatness of each individual person is based on the fact that all human beings share in the greatness of their *name.* Therefore, no individual person will have fullness of life unless all persons – as a community – have fullness of life.

C. The responsibility of becoming instruments for the salvation of humankind

Just as Mary and Joseph accepted the call to join God in his efforts to *"save his people from their sins"* (*Matthew* 1: 21), that is, to save mankind from all forms of destructive antagonism, so too can we all join in the efforts of God and of all who strive to restore unity, equality and justice in the human community.

To join in God's efforts to save humanity means to be totally committed to his plan to save his people. Mary and Joseph demonstrate that kind of commitment by remaining united to each other and to God. Mary and Joseph demonstrate that we cannot claim unity with God unless we live in unity with one another.

Again, he who accepts to restore the human community in the world must fully commit himself to remaining united with his fellow human beings and with God. This task demands a total personal commitment insofar as it means a total communion with the trinitarian God. Mary presents herself as the best example of this type of commitment when she became *"the handmaid of the Lord"* (Luke 1:38). That is to say, Mary, in the plenitude of her freedom, places herself at the service of a God who needs the cooperation from us in order to achieve his plan of salvation and restoration of the human community.

It is, then, appropriate for us to emulate Mary's example, so that we may bring the communitarian God to the world.

How can a human being bring forth God to the world?

This might seem impossible at first. For even Mary, herself, needed to ask the question: *"How can this be, since I have no relations with a man?"* (*Luke* 1:34). This question is not an expression of doubt concerning the power of God, but rather it is a recognition of our human limitations.

Let us ask the same question with different words: How can it be possible for a human being to bring the God of absolute goodness, righteousness and compassion to a world plagued by conflicts and mutual destruction? This might seem to be impossible. But then comes the answer: *"Nothing will be impossible for God"* (*Luke* 1:37). This is the hope and the reality Mary gives us, as the fruit of her womb; this is the hope and the reality we must give to the world, as the fruit of our whole being.

Yes, we need strength in order to bring the Almighty God to the world: *"[God] can strengthen you, according to [the] gospel and the proclamation of Jesus Christ . . . made known to all nations"* (*Romans* 16:25-26). Just as Mary made herself the handmaid of the Lord, we must make ourselves God's cooperators in order to bring forth to the world unity, peace and justice for all.

3. Human quality is measure by the degree of cooperation with God

In the gospel of Luke, Mary is greeted as follows: *"Blessed are you who believed that what was spoken to you by the Lord would be fulfilled"* (*Luke* 1:45). Mary is thus blessed because she cooperated with God taking flesh in her so that he may also take flesh in all human beings. Mary believed the Son of God could be incarnated in her womb, and so it happened. She not only believed that the Son of God had to come to the world, she received him in her body.

Like Mary, we also need to cooperate with God, not only by acknowledging that he is among us, but also by facilitating his work in the world. We need to assert his presence by promoting universal brotherhood, individually and collectively.

By virtue of her cooperation with the Creator, Mary was able, in all justice, to say: *"The Mighty One has done great things for me"* (*Luke* 1:49). Mary, the humble handmaid, the lowly servant of the Lord, becomes the mother of God, the mother of humankind. We too must cooperate with the Almighty so that, in all justice, we may be able to turn our weaknesses into strength, our chains into freedom, and our divisions into unity.

Upon giving birth to Jesus, Mary remained in him and he in her. It is obvious that a pregnant mother is with her child the whole time the child is in her womb. For Mary, the Son of God always remained in her, even after his birth, in the intimate and lasting *mother-son* relationship. Similarly, we all are called to remain united in Jesus if that is the purpose we want for our life.

Fully aware of the Redeemer's will, Mary reaffirms her commitment to collaborate with a God who has *"dispersed the arrogant of mind and heart. He has thrown down the rulers from their thrones but lifted up the lowly. The hungry has filled with good things; the rich he has sent away empty"* (*Luke* 1:51-53).

In order to restore the human community, we too need to cooperate with God in casting down the mighty from their positions of domination, in bringing an end to the destruction of men by men, in filling the starving children of the world with all the good things their human dignity requires, in lifting up all those who suffer oppression, and in sending away, empty, those who appropriate for themselves the wealth that belongs to all.

Since the time of Jesus' conception in his mother's womb, Mary presents herself as the first human being to biologically cooperate with the Trinity, the communitarian God. The relationship between Mary and her son is the model for the relationship between all mothers and their children. Even more, it is the model for the relationship between all human beings.

Mary knows her son, rejoices in her son. Since the very time of conception, Mary knew her son. From the angel of the Lord, she learns that her son's name will be Jesus, the Savior and the Messiah. When she gives birth to her son, Mary is told again, this time by the shepherds of Bethlehem, something she already knew, that her son is *"a savior . . . Messiah and Lord"* (*Luke* 2:11). As a mother, Mary rejoices in the greatness of her son and keeps *"all these things, reflecting on them in her heart"* (*Luke* 2:19). Just as Mary knows and rejoices in her son, we must all know and rejoice in the greatness of each one of us, in the greatness of people who live in *common unity.*

Mary cares for her poor and needy son. The son Mary gives birth to in Bethlehem is a poor, needy infant. She devotes all her life and all her love to him, for he is the fruit of her womb. There was nothing she would not do to protect and care for him. All her son has, is what she can give him. Yet, she has heard and believes that this infant is *a savior . . . the Messiah and Lord.* Therefore, in the poverty and vulnerability of the most defenseless of human beings, Mary sees all the glory and power of God.

The motherhood of Mary is an example calling us to give total care and dedication to all, especially to those who suffer poverty, dispossession, and injustice. For it is in them that the presence of God is made manifest (*Matthew* 25:40).

Chapter IV

A LIGHT REVEALS THE HUMAN COMMUNITY

The light of science and the light of faith assist man in his efforts to understand the Primitive Human Community, which existed in the beginning, and it is now fractured by the conflicts and antagonisms proper to class societies.

Faith and science shed one light, which shines on the world, revealing two realities: on the one hand, the goodness of God consisting in communitarian life, and on the other hand, human transgressions consisting in the breakup of human unity.

– The goodness of God

God comes to the world in Jesus as a king to govern his *people with justice, to defend the oppressed among the people, save the poor and crush the oppressor (Psalm 72: 4). "He shows pity to the needy and the poor and saves the lives of the poor. From extortion and violence he frees them, for precious is their blood in his sight"* (Psalm 72: 13-14). Behold the goodness of God: Jesus Christ comes to the world as a ruler who shepherds his people through the path of justice and peace, whose rule is based on unity and respect for all, as a ruler who gives his life for his people in the same way a shepherd gives his life for his sheep.

All the power of God is initially made flesh in the person of a child – the child Jesus. The power of God is revealed and resides in the innocence, sincerity, and vulnerability of a child. *"On entering the house [the magi] saw the child with Mary his mother"* (*Matthew* 2:11).

– Human transgressions

In the gospel of Matthew, king Herod – the ruling power of the time – is presented as the embodiment of human transgressions. Upon learning of the presence of a new King, Herod *"was greatly troubled, and all Jerusalem with him"* (*Matthew* 2:3). He then said to the magi, *"Go and search diligently for the child. When you have found him, bring me word, that I too may go and do him homage"* (*Matthew* 2:8).

Demonstrating utmost political hypocrisy, Herod pretends to be willing to accept the new order when, in fact, he wants to destroy it, he pretends to welcome Jesus when, in fact, he wants to kill him.

Throughout history, humanity has witnessed the presence of individuals who have followed the model of God, while others have followed the model of Herod. The light will allow us to see them as they are.

1. The light of the communitarian God allows us to know ourselves and the world

In order to know the human community, man must first know himself, individually, because a community is the product of the sum of its members. We come to know ourselves when God gives light to our eyes and courage to our will. Our efforts to change the world may prove fruitless if we fail to summon the light and the courage of God.

When God made himself man in Jesus, he came as the light of the world so we may see and know our world under his light. This light allows us to see the following:

- The antagonisms in the world and in us.
- The need to eradicate said antagonisms.
- The true benefits inherent in the human community wherein men live in peace and harmony.

The world will not be wonderful until we come to see it under the light of the Redeemer, and rebuild it in is original form as a human community under the light of the Creator. In the beginning, the Creator said, *"Let there be light,' and there was light"* (*Genesis* 1:3). And, the human community was the first thing man saw. When men destroyed the community, Jesus came to us as the light – the light that dispels the darkness of antagonism and division. The world, however, offers stern resistance to receiving the light.

The light of God is as effective at the time it was first created as when it was manifested in the form of an infant child in Bethlehem. The light of God will prevail over darkness; that is to say, justice will prevail over injustice, peace will prevail over war, unity over division, and life over death.

Just as the light of creation made life possible on earth, so the light of Jesus makes our peaceful coexistence possible in the universal human community.

Peaceful coexistence requires a commitment to unity

Peaceful coexistence would be an illusory aspiration if men lacked the capacity to commit themselves to living in unity with themselves and with their Creator. Such unity involves a communication between God and men, between heaven and earth, a heaven with doors that can be opened from earth so that a continuity between earthy life and eternal life may be established. The gospel of Matthew says: *"After Jesus was baptized, he came up from the water and behold, the heavens were opened"* (*Matthew* 3:16).

When Christ comes to the world, he announces the end of injustices among people, he *brings forth justice to the nations; he brings the victory of justice because he is a light for the nations* (*Isaiah* 42:1-6). Indeed, his work is *"to open the eyes of the blind, to bring out prisoners from confinement, and from the dungeon, those who live in darkness"* (*Isaiah* 42:7). That is how the God incarnate opens the doors of heaven from earth.

We need to keep the heavens open

Just as the Lord Jesus opens the doors of heaven by his justice and righteousness, so we too ought to do likewise. Once heaven is opened, it is up to us to keep it open by continuing the works of the Redeemer on earth; thus, the Father will be *"well pleased"* (*Matthew* 3:17) with us.

We keep the doors of heaven open by living in peace on earth, by eliminating the divisions among men, and by ending injustices and mutual destruction, which so deeply afflict humanity. Just as God *"proclaimed peace through Jesus Christ"* (*Acts* 10:36), so too we need to proclaim it to the world today. God needs us to go about *"doing good and healing all those oppressed by the devil"* (*Acts* 10: 38), healing and bringing liberation to those who are oppressed by the evils of the world, oppressed by those who disregard the equality of human nature.

Those who fail to bring forth unity among men, close the doors of heaven.

We are dealing with a monumental challenge, but its success is availed by the Almighty's involvement, for he is with us every day; and each day is an opportunity for us to respond to him, to express our commitment to remain in him and to conform to his generous plan in favor of the human community. Therefore, each day is a day of baptism in God. Each day, he gives us his Spirit so we may carry out his will: *"Here is my servant . . . upon whom I have put my spirit; he shall bring forth justice to the nations"* (*Isaiah* 42:1).

Jesus' mission is also our mission because the baptism the Father confers upon Jesus, he also confers upon us so we may carry out his will and bring about *"the victory of justice"* (*Isaiah* 42:6).

Our baptism in Jesus is a call for each one of us to *"open the eyes of the blind, to bring out prisoners from confinement, and from the dungeon, those who live in darkness"* (*Isaiah* 42:7). Therefore, to be baptized in Christ Jesus means to become his followers, the witnesses he needs, so the world may see in us a people living in common unity, for *"whenever two or more gather in my name, I am in their midst"* (*Matthew* 18:20).

To be baptized in God means to fully receive his light and to adhere to the belief that he is in all human beings, without exception (otherwise there is no belief in God), for *"God shows no partiality. Rather, in every nation whoever fears him and acts uprightly is acceptable to him"* (*Acts* 10:34, 35).

The baptism of Jesus is a revelation that God is in every human being, that God has come to the world, not only to demonstrate his unity with men, but also to guide humans to living in unity with one another. It is for this reason that humanity is baptized in the name of the Father, the Son, and the Holy Spirit; that is, in the name of three Persons who establish an unbreakable unity between them: the unity of one and indivisible God. Thus, our own baptism must produce unity between all of us; otherwise, we are not baptized in God.

Our world seems to be far away from that baptism of unity on account of the divisions prevalent among humans. Just as the baptism of Jesus marks the beginning of his public ministry, so should our own baptism mark the beginning of unity among all human beings.

2. Divisive actions and the victory of unity

As indicated in previous chapters, the Primitive Human Community was fractured into antagonistic socioeconomic classes by the actions of small groups of individuals who, moved by their greed to accumulate wealth, appropriated for themselves the goods belonging to the community. The Book of Genesis explains that the fragmentation of the human community was the result of humans' disobedience to the will of their Creator. Genesis points out that human beings (Adam and Eve) fell into the temptation of believing that the life of God (that is, the life of unity between humans and their unity with God) was "not good enough" for humanity.

Thus, those who originally lived as communitarian beings came to realize they were different from one another *"and they realized that they were naked"* (*Genesis* 3:7), learned that they did not share in the same dignity and, therefore, could take advantage of one another and even destroy one another. They turned from unity to division, from equality to inequality. And division and inequality became the norm.

In the primordial state of human life, sin did not manifest itself because *"sin is not accounted when there is no law"* (*Romans* 5:13). There was no law because people lived in unity among themselves and in unity with God. The life of unity, however, was broken when *"through the disobedience of one person the many were made sinners"* (*Romans* 5:19), heirs of a disobedience consisting in the rejection of the unity established by the Creator. Thus, the power of the world took over the power of God; and humankind became divided.

Nowadays, the powerful of the world continue to defy the will of the Creator inasmuch as they believe that the unity (instituted by God) is *no good* for humanity.

In the gospel of Matthew 4:1-11, the tempter subjects Jesus to several temptations presented under the form of propositions leading to divide men, and separate them from God.

The following are the actions of those who fall under divisive temptations:

- The tempter says to Jesus (and, to all men) *"command that these stones become loaves of bread"* (*Matthew* 4:3). And that is precisely what those who pursue the wealth of the world do. They appropriate for themselves the wealth produced for the common good, and accumulate it for their own selfish interests. He who pursues the wealth of the world turns into **his** what belongs to everybody, and appropriates for himself the *"loaves of bread"* as if they were *"stones"* turned into bread. The one who appropriates for himself the bread produced by others, eats the bread without working, just as the one who *commands the stones to become loaves of bread* eats without working.
- The tempter tells them, *"Throw [yourselves] down... For [God] will command his angels concerning you and with their hands they will support you, lest you dash your foot against a stone"* (*Matthew* 4:6). In other words, the tempter tells them to throw themselves behind policies that perpetuate division and injustice, for God will not allow any harm to befall them. And that is precisely what those who promote injustice do. They perpetuate division under the assumption that God will not permit their destruction.
- The tempter tells them, *"All these [the kingdoms of the world] I shall give to you, if you will prostrate yourself and worship me"* (*Matthew*

4:9). And that is precisely what those who seek the power of the world do. They prostrate themselves and worship the "idols" of dominion and power, which are the means they use to control the world.

The following are the victories of those who promote unity

- First victory: *"man does not live on bread alone, but by every word that comes forth from the mouth of God"* (*Matthew* 4:4). Unity, peace, justice, and love of neighbor are the words that come out of the mouth of God. They are the true food that makes men develop and grow. Once people take such food, they will be able to use material wealth in accordance with its true purpose, which is to serve the needs of all.
- Second victory: men must *"not put the Lord, your God, to the test"* (*Matthew* 4:7). That is to say, we cannot expect God to tolerate our abusive power. For the time will come when those who fail to change their abusive ways, will meet with their own obliteration.
- Third victory: man is to worship and serve the Lord, our God (*Matthew* 4:10). We must reject the gods of power and accumulation of wealth. We serve God by serving our fellowmen, by respecting the bonds of unity among us.

The victory of unity over division is a victory for humanity.

3. The attacks against unity are attacks against human rights

These attacks against human rights present themselves in the form of temptations. **What human rights are under attack?**

- **The first right: the right to satisfy our needs.** The Creator has given us the right to satisfy our needs to the fullest and in accordance with our human dignity. That is, all persons, individually and collectively, have the power to earn, through their work, what they need to live.

The attack against this right takes the form of the following temptation: *"If you are the Son of God, command this stone to become bread" (Luke 4:3)*. This temptation is an attempt to lure us into obtaining our "bread" by means other than those established by God. To command a *"stone to become bread"* is a way of saying that I have the power to make mine the bread I have not worked for (or even the bread that belongs to others).

Jesus' answer to this attack is: *"One does not live by bread alone" (Luke 4:4)* meaning that we are to live in accordance with the order established by God. That is, we are to satisfy our needs through our individual and collective work (as a human race), not by depriving others of what they produce and need.

The powerful socioeconomic classes have fallen to the first temptation. We live in a world where small groups have appropriated for themselves the "bread" (the goods) that has been produced by others, the "bread" the producers need to live on.

– **The second right: the right to the proper use of power.** Inasmuch as the Almighty shares his power with us, we have the right to use such power in order to dominate what God has created for us.

The attack against this right takes the form of the following temptation: the devil showed Jesus all the kingdoms of the world in a single instance, and said, *"I shall give you all this power and their glory . . . if you worship me" (Luke 4:5-7)*. This temptation is an attempt to lure us into giving up the power that comes from God (based on unity and equality) and replace it with the power that is based on domination and oppression. The power to abuse and oppress is intrinsically evil.

Jesus' answer to this temptation, *"You shall worship the Lord, your God, and him alone shall you serve" (Luke 4:8)* is a reaffirmation that the only power that builds humanity (in "soul" and "body") comes from God, a power, which frees us from oppression and injustice. This answer reaffirms that whenever men live in unity and mutual respect, they are worshiping and serving God, their creator and redeemer.

The powerful of the world have fallen to the second temptation insofar as they use their power in order to serve their own interests.

-   **The third right: the right to the truth.** God is the truth that is revealed to us throughout history and is now here among us, liberating us from injustice, and motivating us to restore the human community. God is the truth that sets us free, the truth that belong to humanity since the beginning.

    The attack against this right takes the form of the following temptation: *"If you are the Son of God, throw yourself down from here, for it is written: he will command his angels concerning you, to guard you, and with their hands they will support you, lest you dash your foot against a stone"* (*Luke* 4:9, 10). This temptation is an attempt to lure us into believing that the falsehoods of the world are better than God's truth. This temptation tries to lure us away from our responsibilities to cooperate with God (through our own cross and resurrection) in restoring unity in humankind.

    Jesus' answer to this temptation: *"'You shall not put the Lord, your God, to the test'"* (*Luke* 4: 12) means that men will not be lured into denying their identity as children of God. This answer reaffirms the truth that we ought to remain faithful to our relationship with the communitarian God.

    Presently, the powerful ruling elites of the world have fallen to the third temptation because they distort the truth by presenting injustices and inequalities as if they were the norm. Many people seem to be satisfied with this lie, and are reluctant to take their cross to restore God's truth, and return to a life of *common unity.*

4. There is a way to prevent humanity from being destroyed by division

"Repent" (*Mark* 1:15).

Repentance is needed because the enemy of unity is actively at work in our world preventing us from restoring our human unity and equality, preventing us from living in peace with one another, and from reaching fullness of life – individually and collectively.

What is repentance?

Repentance is the action by which a person transforms the destructive effects of divisiveness into unifying forces. That is, through repentance, a person returns to the unity initially intended by the Creator for all human beings. It is a return to the freedom of the children of God. It is an action which transforms death into life. Repentance transforms the suffering that ends in destruction into the redemption that brings about life.

As repentance leads to unity among men, it becomes a source of joy. The joy of the fulfillment of the promise: the promise of fullness of life, the promise made by the Redeemer to all of us. Through repentance, we cleanse ourselves individually and collectively from chaos and antagonisms, just as the floodwaters cleansed the world in Noah's time. Through repentance, we will renew our commitment to God and restore peace and unity among us *so that the waters shall never again become a flood to destroy all mortal beings*" (*Genesis* 9:15).

Chapter V

THE GREATNESS OF
HUMAN NATURE

1. The greatness of human nature according to God's revelation

The New Testament reveals the greatness of human nature in the event of the Transfiguration of Jesus Christ. When God became man in Jesus, he showed his nature for human eyes to see: *"his face shone like the sun and his clothes became white as light"* (*Matthew* 17:2). It is God's trustworthiness, his love for justice, and his goodness that *makes his face shine like the sun and his clothes white as light.*

If human nature did not have the potential to "shine like the sun," God would not have become a man.

Consequently, we can rescue our human nature if we free ourselves from the darkness of division and inequality, making it again *shine like the sun and white as light.* We are capable of doing this because our human nature is the depository of God's attributes, that is, the depository of a God whose *"word is true; all his works are trustworthy;"* a God who *"loves justice and right, and fills the earth with goodness"* (*Psalm* 33:4-5).

However, the destructive antagonisms among men have degraded human nature so much so that it appears to be almost impossible for us to restore the goodness the Creator instilled in us since the beginning.

The restoration of the goodness of our human nature

In order to restore the goodness of our human nature, we must follow these steps:

- We must believe that God is united to our human nature. God speaks of this unity when he says, *"This is my beloved Son"* (*Matthew* 17:5). This means that each and every human being is united with God. And it is because of this unity that human nature shares in the brightness and light of God.
- We must accept that human nature reaches its fullness when it is united with the trinitarian God. Since we are all children of God, he is *"well pleased"* (*Matthew* 17:5) with us all. There is nothing that could better define the greatness of human nature than its unity with God, inasmuch as unity pleases the Almighty.
- *We must listen to the Father,* for by doing so, we become his children, just like his Only Son.

Now, to be God's children involves sharing in the *"hardship for the gospel with the strength that comes from God"* (*2 Timothy* 1:8). For it is inevitable that those who side with God in the struggle against the divisive forces of the world will *shine like the sun and become white as light.* Furthermore, those who aspire to partake in the qualities of Jesus (that is, those who share in his transfiguration) will be freed from all forms of evil. For they have been called by God to share in his life *"according to his own design and the grace bestowed on us in Christ Jesus before time began"* (*2 Timothy* 1:9).

By virtue of our union with Jesus, we become protagonists of the restoration of the greatness of human nature, and heirs of God's power and support. *"If God is for us, who can be against us? He who did not spare his only Son but handed him over for us all, how will he not also give us everything else along with him"* (*Romans* 8:31-32). He will give us the crown of unity, the blessing of peace, and the glory of universal justice.

God makes himself man so we may see him as he truly is, so we may see in him the radiance proper to his nature. The radiant God is an invitation for all human beings to take on his radiance.

Through his transfiguration in front of human eyes, Jesus reveals to us his life. A life we will share with him once we become liberated from the dehumanizing conflicts of the world. A liberation which Christ *"was going to accomplish in Jerusalem"* (*Luke* 9:31) through his cross and resurrection.

The image of the radiant God in his transfiguration is the image of a liberated humanity, the image of humanity living in *common unity*, living to the fullest. The transfiguration of Jesus Christ is a way for him to tell us that he *"will change our lowly body to conform to his glorified body"* (*Philippians* 3:21).

While some people refuse to be changed into the glorified body of God, others are willing to do so.

- Those who refuse *"conduct themselves as enemies of the cross of Christ . . . Their god is their stomach; their glory is their shame"* (*Philippians* 3:18-19). *"Their god is their stomach"* means that their god is greed, accumulated of wealth. They resort to all sorts of wrongdoings in order to satisfy their *stomachs*. *"Their glory is their shame"* means that their wrongdoings are their glorious deeds. What they consider their glory is actually their shame in the eyes of God and men.
- Those who are willing to be transformed into the glorified body of God, *"conduct themselves according to the model [God reveals to] us"* (*Philippians* 3:17), the model of unity and equality, the model of the savior, the model of a God always trinitarian, always communitarian.

2. Communitarian life is like water satisfying our thirst for unity

Just as human life is not possible without water, so the human community is not possible without unity. From a physical point of view, it goes without saying that we need water to live, and whenever there is a deficit of water in our body, we experience thirst – the distressful urge caused by our unmet need for water. The longer the need goes unmet, the more painful it becomes, and it will eventually lead to death if there is no intake of water within a given time.

It can also be said that if the human body receives the water it needs in a constant and systematic manner, the person will not experience the distressful feeling of thirst. Thus, an appropriate supply of water will keep the feeling of thirst under control. However, once water is withheld, thirst signals that the need has reappeared.

Just like the proper use of an inexhaustible supply of water prevents the onset of thirst, a similarly inexhaustible supply of, say, food will prevent the onset of hunger. The same principle applies to all human needs; that is, once a need is satisfied, that need ceases for the moment. Once human beings find a way to properly and fully satisfy their needs, then we can say they have found a way to eliminate the suffering resulting from unmet needs.

Something similar occurs with the human need to live in unity. The lack of unity among men causes them to live in a state of fragmentation, amid destructive conflicts which can only be remedied with the restoration of the communitarian way of life.

Jesus is the living water and *"whoever drinks the water I shall give will never thirst"* (*John* 4:14).

What is this living water? It is the caring commitment that bonds men with one another, and prompts them to mutually meet their needs (physical and spiritual) in a manner that frees them from experiencing the destructive effects of unmet needs – physical or spiritual.

An example that clarifies the concept of the *living water* is the commitment parents make to their children. Through their efforts, work, and sacrifice, parents ensure that their child's needs do not go unmet, thus, rendering the child's needs practically inexistent because they are properly and timely satisfied.

The parents' unselfish care, loving commitment, and unconditional dedication constitute the spring of living water that satisfies the needs of their children. And the children, through the example of their parents, learn not only to receive, but also to give such living water. Therefore, parents and children can rejoice together because the living water flows between them from generation to generation.

This living water also flows between people working toward their common welfare: *"The sower and the reaper can rejoice together" for they are "sharing the fruits of their work"* (*John* 4:36, 38).

How does man satisfy his hunger and thirst for God? *By doing the will of God and finishing his work* (*John* 4:34), thus, the will of God and our work are the fountain of *living water.* Man's work consists of giving humanity the ability to live in a world where people properly and fully meet their needs. Furthermore, our thirst of unity with God includes also our thirst of unity with our fellow human beings. It is Christ himself who comes to quench our thirst for living water, *"whoever drinks the water I shall give will never thirst"* (*John* 4:14).

Consequently, doing God's will includes doing whatever is necessary in order to give humanity the capacity of living in a communitarian world, wherein every person has the right to possess the necessary means to meet his needs. However, class societies have turned the possession of goods (whose sole and proper use is the satisfaction of everybody's needs) into the privilege of a few, causing many people to starve, to suffer disease, to be dispossessed of what they produce and forced to live in subhuman conditions.

Just as our body needs water to live, so does everybody need peace and unity to reach fullness of life; that is, we all need the living water, which allows us to live as wholesome human beings. However, humanity is dying of "thirst" because man deprives man of the living water he needs to live.

Inasmuch as the human community is a design of the Creator, he shares his living water with us. In turn, we must share it with all: among individuals, among collectivities, satisfying everyone's needs (physical and spiritual) at the highest level required by our human dignity. Thus, each person becomes *"a spring of water welling up to eternal life"* (*John* 4:14).

3. Living in community defines the characteristics of human greatness

Life in community, rationally organized, is our distinctive human characteristic; it is what makes man a human being. Saint Paul, in his

Letter to the Ephesians, defines human beings as *"children of light [who produce] every kind of goodness and righteousness and truth"* (*Ephesians* 5:8-9). Living in community allows us to be who we are, namely:

We are good by nature (as opposed to being evil by nature). For we fulfill ourselves by producing "every kind of goodness." No one who is evil can produce good fruits.

We are righteous because our nature allows us to realize justice in our lives and in our relations with one another by placing the interest of everybody else before our own individual interests. We are righteous because human justice is the product of our own volition, not of an external imposition.

We are truthful. For we define ourselves by what we are (as opposed to what we are not). Human truth is the correspondence between who we are and how we live; that is, we live in truth whenever we relate to one another as members of a community, not divided into antagonistic classes.

Does the world see what makes us human?

Evidently, it does not. The world refuses to see what makes us human each time it denies our goodness, righteousness, and truth. Whenever we fail to live in accordance with what makes us human, that is, whenever we fail to live in accordance with our goodness, righteousness, and truth we become less than human, we become *"darkness"* (*Ephesians* 5:8).

The world chooses to remain in darkness:

A. The world only looks at appearances, *not into the heart*. God, on the contrary, looks into the heart: *"Not as man [the world] sees does God see, because man sees the appearance but the Lord looks into the heart"* (*1 Samuel* 16:7). The world is satisfied with seeing the *appearances* of its own making; for instance, the world sees as "justice" what is only a mockery of justice; the world sees as "order" what in fact is chaos; the world sees as "rebuilding" what in reality is only destruction; the world sees as "life" what in actuality is death; as "unity" what in fact is fragmentation. The end result of these appearances is *darkness*.

B. The world rejects those who *see* what they truly are, those who strive at unity for humankind. It rejects those who live in accordance with their goodness, righteousness, and truth. It rejects those who live in accordance with the attributes given them by God.

C. Those who hold economic, political, military or any other type of power, pretend to reduce men to a permanent state of inequality and oppression. In the eyes of those who hold worldly power, the person who suffers oppression should always remain under oppression, as if oppression were the "normal" state of human life. The oppressor says to the oppressed, *"You were born totally in sin"* (*John* 9:34).

4. Passing from division to unity is like passing from death to life

The breakup of unity among men is, in a way, something similar to a death. Jesus, however proclaims his power over death: *"Whoever believes in me, even if he dies, will live, and everyone who lives and believes in me will never die"* (*John* 11:25-26). It is a power of which men are the beneficiaries: *"If the Spirit of the one who raised Jesus from the dead dwells in you, the one who raised Christ from the dead will give life to your mortal bodies also, through his Spirit that dwells in you"* (*Romans* 8:11).

Now, we ask:

A. Who are those who do not have the Spirit of God?

They are those who live *"in the flesh"* (*Romans* 8:8). That is, those who live a life in opposition to the life Christ brought to the world. They live in contradiction to the order established by the Creator, an order based on and realized in the unity and harmony among all men.

"The concern of the flesh is death" (*Romans* 8:6), is a disorderly and selfish existence. It is the kind of existence that not only destroys

the *body*, but also annihilates the efforts of the Spirit to dwell in the *body*. *"Those who are in the flesh"* are the ones who promote division, antagonism, and destruction among men.

B. Who are those who have the Spirit of God?

They are those who promote justice, peace and unity; in other words, those who live *"in the Spirit"* (*Romans* 8:9). Under these circumstances, *"the Spirit of God dwells"* in them (*Romans* 8:11) because *"the concern of the Spirit is life and peace"* (*Romans* 8:6).

It follows that our mortal body has true life only by virtue of the Spirit dwelling in it; and the absence of the Spirit leaves us with an empty body, a body without life. Therefore, any human collectivity without the Spirit will be a contradiction of true human life.

The world rejects the Spirit of God

The mutual destruction among men renders our world empty of the Spirit of God, a world living *"in the flesh," and the "concern of the flesh is death."*

Because a divided world is in opposition to the Spirit of God, it is an "empty world," which can only resort, as in fact it does, to an adoration of what is temporal, such as material wealth and earthly power. The world of the flesh begets and belittles the oppressed, the poor, the suffering, the ill, and the disenfranchised (who are precisely the product of the injustices and selfishness prevalent in the world).

In a world where the body is everything, the death of the body is the end of everything. Thus, those who live in the flesh are left with emptiness. The world of the flesh has buried peace in the tomb of war, justice in the tomb of injustice, equality in the tomb of inequality, and unity in the tomb of division.

We must instill the Spirit of God in our world by bringing about *"life and peace"* (*Romans* 8:6). Once the Spirit of God is instilled in each individual and manifested in the life of the entire human community, we will bring true life and peace to the world, we will bring the world out of its tomb, and back into life.

Just as Jesus commands, *"Lazarus, come out!"* (*John* 11:43), so must we command:

- "Peace, come out!" And peace will come out of the tomb of war.
- "Justice, come out!" And justice will come out of the tomb of injustice.
- "Equality, come out!" And equality will come out of the tomb of inequality.
- "Unity, come out!" And unity will come out of the tomb of division.

Once we allow the Spirit of God to live in us, we will be able to say: "World come out!" And the world will come out of its tomb of death.

Chapter VI

THE HUMAN COMMUNITY
IS LIKE A TEMPLE

The human community is like a temple which remains standing up when its members live in unity. However, whenever unity breaks up, the temple collapses and it becomes necessary to rebuild it. Indeed, it becomes our responsibility to rebuild the body of humanity just as Jesus Christ makes every effort in order to rebuild the Temple of his body, the temple of humanity.

When men abuse or degrade other men (the temple of God), Jesus drives out of the temple *those who turn it into a marketplace* (*John* 2:16), those who desecrate the temple of humankind by turning it into a place where money and material possessions have more value than human beings.

At the individual level, any person who rebuilds himself from the ruins caused by division and conflict is restoring his own being – a *temple of the Holy Spirit*. Whatever the case may be, we all have the responsibility to rebuild humanity, to rebuild the body of God with total commitment and zeal: *"Zeal for your house will consume me"* (*John* 2:17).

But those who exploit their fellow human beings object by saying: *"What sign can you show us for doing this?"* (*John* 2:18). Those who refuse to accept that humanity is the temple God try to deny that he lives in us all; they want to believe that God and humanity are the possession of a reduced group of people.

Since God created the world to be the possession of all human beings, we ought to rebuild it every time it is destroyed by those who appropriate for themselves what belongs to all: *"Destroy this temple and in three days I will raise it up"* (*John* 2:19).

As our world becomes increasingly desecrated and destroyed by those who promote injustice and oppression, by those who are moved by the greed of money and world domination, God shows powerful *signs* that will bring about the rebuilding of the human community, the temple of humanity, the Temple of God. Behold the *signs*: living in unity as members of one body, renouncing anything that causes division and oppression among ourselves.

1. Every injustice exposes the structural deficiencies of the temple

Every injustice produces a victim and every victim is a denunciation against the unjust. That is, the one who suffers injustice exposes the harm perpetrated by the unjust. The victim of any injustice resembles the Son of Man who was *lifted up on a cross* (*John* 3:14) for everybody to see.

The perpetrators of injustice can no longer hide because:

A. Their victims are a visible denunciation of the harm inflicted by the perpetrators.

B. The perpetrators of injustice, usually act in the name of a "legitimate" societal order that, openly or subtlety, promotes or condones injustice.

Once the victim is *lifted up on his cross*, injustice can no longer hide, can no longer disguise itself under the cover of false "legitimacy" or fake "righteousness", because the victim, the image and likeness of God, is up there for everybody to see. The redemption of the suffering humanity is at hand, since the victim we see lifted up on the cross is the Son of God, who denounces injustice, and invites us to rebuild a human community based on justice, peace and unity.

Just as Christ allows us to see him on the cross, he also allows us to see him as a risen Lord so that we may know what he stands for, and how to join him. To those who want to see Christ, he allows them to see everything about him (*John* 12: 20-33). Since we are the image and likeness of God, whenever we see him, we see us in him; a God who is a creator and redeemer, a God-made-man who shares with us his glory, which consists of the triumph of unity over fragmentation, justice over injustice, life over death: *"The hour has come for the Son of Man to be glorified"* (*John* 12:23).

Everybody is invited to join him in the struggle between division and unity, between death and life, and the ultimate victory of the latter. To see Christ means to become a *"grain of wheat [which] falls to the ground and dies"* so it may *"produce much fruit"* (*John* 12:24).

Those who want to see Jesus Christ must be willing to commit themselves to the radical transformation he stands for, to be willing to restore the human community in such a way that everyone may live in unity and equality, leaving behind the individual and social antagonisms that are so prevalent in and glorified by our world.

When someone is willing to make this commitment, he will bring a great deal of trials and difficulties into his life, but will preserve it for eternal life. However, he who promotes injustice, division, and selfish power on earth, may lead a wonderful worldly life but, in the end, he will not reach life eternal (*John* 12:25) because injustice cannot be continued to eternal life.

What does it mean to restore the temple of the human community?

It means to return to living in accordance with our human dignity, that is to say, living in a way that every person places the welfare of others before his own, and nobody causes any harm upon another.

On the contrary, to live in violation of our human dignity is to live a life whereby men are divided into antagonistic groups, a life whereby some individuals appropriate for themselves as much wealth as they can while the victims of dispossession are left in poverty.

Now, we may ask: Are the victims of dispossession the ones who will perish? By no means! The ones who exploit their fellowmen are the ones who will perish *"if [they] do not repent"* (*Luke* 13:5). Those who exploit others will perish because the exploitation of man by man is an offense against God. The death of the victim of exploitation is a death in the flesh but not in the spirit because the spirit always remains alert and ready to engage in the restauration of unity and justice among the people. Whereas the death of the exploiter is a death in the spirit, even though he may continue his earthly existence in the flesh.

Those who promote division will perish if they *do not repent* (*Luke* 13:5). Repentance, therefore, is the means by which the unjust can return to a state of unity and equality with their fellow human beings.

The return to a state of common unity is what allows a person to bear fruit, just like a tree bears fruit when it is well taken care of. We must *cultivate our world so that "it may bear fruit in the future"* (*Luke* 13:8, 9), so that it may bear fruit for humankind; otherwise, it will be cut down.

2. A prodigal son who causes separation and destruction

Just like the temple of community can be torn down by separation among its members, so can it happen with the temple of the family. Separation is the most effective way to destroy both community and family. In the parable of the Prodigal Son, the evangelist Luke tells the story of a son who upon separating himself from his family causes it to become incomplete, and brings about harm to its members.

What is the cause of this separation? in other words, what causes the prodigal son to break the unity of his family? The cause is greed for the wealth coming to him from his father, wealth, which will allow the son to live a life of dissipation and licentiousness. The son believes that with "his" wealth, he can have a "better" life, a "life of dissipation", and that that life is more important to him than the life of unity in his family.

The prodigal son' experience can be applied to a collectivity

The person who appropriates for himself the wealth of his fellowmen, or in any way inflicts harm upon others, is responsible for destroying the unity among men and making humankind incomplete.

The loss of unity is the *"state of sin"* that those who promote separation immerse our world in; it is the *"state of sin"* in which the prodigal son lives while he leads a life of dissipation.

The restoration of unity in the family of the prodigal son

What did the prodigal son do in order to restore the unity of his family? He came to the realization that his life in a *"distant country"* far away from his family was not better than the life with his family. Therefore, *"coming to his senses,"* he decided to return to his family (*Luke* 15:17-18). The son knew the solution was in his hands.

Similarly, he who separates himself from his fellow human beings needs to come "to his senses" and realize that the life of separation he imposes upon others is not better than the life whereby all men live in unity. However, the *life of dissipation* led by those who destroy unity is, indeed, too attractive to give up unless, of course, "a severe famine" strikes and makes them come to their senses.

The return of the prodigal son is a cause of joy. The father joyfully celebrates the return of his lost son because the unity of his family has been restored, because his family has become once again wholesome. The separation of the prodigal son meant a death; his return meant life. And, the restoration of unity and the rebirth of life are always occasions for celebration. *"Let us celebrate with a feast"* (*Luke* 15: 23).

Just like the break-up of the unity within a family is the result of the separation of one or more of its members, so is the break-up of the unity within a collectivity. In both cases, the restoration of unity will be in the hands of the individual or group that caused the separation. Obviously, the task of restoration of the unity in a class society will be more complicated than the restoration of unity in a family.

Why is the restoration of unity more complicated in a class society?

Because the divisions in a class society are usually protected by the law. History shows that, in a class society, the state of division between strong and weak, rich and poor is consolidated by a legal system necessary to maintain the established "order".

A person, who abides by such legal system may (externally) appear to be virtuous when (in his conscience) he is not. Those who conduct themselves in accordance with the laws concerning socioeconomic divisions, may appear to be righteous before the eyes of class society, while, in actually, they are acting against the unity instituted by the Creator.

Chapter VII

THE RESTORATION OF UNITY
IS A FORM OF LIBERATION

There are times in human history when man lives (physically or mentally) in the form of a slave, which is a form radically different than that in which he was originally created.

Men take the form of slaves by their own doing, namely:

- By imposing upon one another a way of life based on injustice and oppression.
- By failing to see one another as children of God.
- By failing to respect the bonds of unity, peace, and mutual support among themselves.
- By failing to seek their common good.

Into this world, God, made man in Jesus, came in order to liberate it, in order, to restore man to the form in which he was originally created. When God came to the world, humanity was in a state of slavery, so God had to take the form of a slave. For a slave is any human being who lives in a world of injustice and oppression: *"Christ Jesus, who though he was in the form of God, did not regard equality with God something to be grasped. Rather, he emptied himself, taking the form of a slave, coming in human likeness"* (*Philippians* 2:5-7).

The liberation of humankind is the fruit of the sacrifices made by Christ himself, it is the expression of his infinite love for all human beings, a love, which brings about true liberation in every aspect of human life, both in body and in soul. Men, in turn, join Christ in the task of liberation by fostering communitarian life, peace, and justice for all.

The triumphal entrance of Jesus to Jerusalem makes visible the nature of the liberation he brings to the world, a liberation to be accomplished through the power of God, not through the power of the world. Let us highlight the radical differences between the way Jesus liberates and the way the world "liberates."

A. Jesus liberates by humbly obeying the will of the Father, by adhering to righteousness, and by respecting all human beings. His power does not lead him to belittle, oppress, destroy, lie, or impose his authority over others. Jesus – the Son of the Almighty – enters Jerusalem *meek and riding on an ass, an on a colt, the foal of a beast of burden"* (*Matthew* 21:5). In other words, Jesus reveals his liberating power through humility.

B. The world, on the contrary, pretends to "liberate" men by enticing them to seek their own self-interests and their own wellbeing at the expense of their fellow human beings' best interests. Under this approach, no liberation is accomplished, but rather it leads men into deeper slavery. This is how the power of the world operates:

– By institutionalizing domination, if not the outright destruction of one by the other.
– By encouraging the use of force (brute or otherwise) by the strong against the weak.

As Jesus showed his liberating power *by entering into Jerusalem meek and riding on an ass, the foal of the beast of burden,* so too must we set aside all forms of domination and demonstrate readiness to serve and respect one another. For that is the true way to achieve liberation.

1. Liberation is a manifestation of the power of God

In order to reveal his power, the Second Person of the Trinity makes himself weak, as weak as the lowliest servant, so the weak of the world may become strong and free, as God is strong and free. Jesus *"emptied himself, taking the form of a slave, . . . becoming obedient to death, even death on a cross. Because of this, God greatly exalted him"* (*Philippians* 2:7-9). Sharing in the power of God, the power to make us servants of all, makes us pleasing to God.

It was the power of Jesus on the cross that led him to his triumph over death. We, human beings, must also resort to the power of God in order to triumph over oppression and division. For the power of God remains within us always, even in our weakness – especially in our weakness.

The power of the world collides against the power of God

This is how the power of the world expresses itself:

– *"The kings of the Gentiles lord it over them and those in authority over them are addressed as 'Benefactors'; but among you it shall not be so. Rather, let the greatest among you be as the youngest, and the leader as the servant"* (*Luke* 22:25-26). The leaders of the world do not tolerate any other form of power than that which is forcefully imposed upon people.

– Worldly powers conspire against Christ, the liberator: *"Herod and Pilate [The political and military institutions] became friends that very day, even though they had been enemies formerly"* (*Luke* 23:12).

– The power of the world temporarily seizes the power of God: *"Day after day I was with you in the temple area, and you did not seize me; but this is your hour, the time for the power of darkness"* (*Luke* 22:53), the time when injustice and oppression rule over the world.

In brief, while the power of the world expresses itself in men's capacity to exploit one another, the power of God is manifested in men's capacity to restore the human community so that everybody may live in unity and peace.

2. The triumphant power

The resurrection of Jesus Christ is the summit of the triumph of God's power over the power of the world, the triumph of life over death, of communitarian unity over class division, of freedom over subjugation. Just as the restoration of unity implies that there, previously, was division, so does the restoration of life imply that there, previously, was a death. Those who were divided are now united. The one who was dead is now alive. That is the nature of the power of God.

The death of Jesus sets the groundwork for his resurrection

In the tomb, Jesus is the victim killed by the injustices, the fratricidal conflicts among men, the wrongs of the world. In the tomb he denounces the actions of a world that rejects unity, a world that cannot accept the life God came to bring to mankind, a world intent on destroying the goodness belonging to humankind.

The world today appears determined to remain in the tomb by encouraging selfishness, promoting the glorification of the powerful and the subjugation of the weak, and fostering conflicts between individuals and between nations. Those are the reasons our world is determined to remain in the tomb.

While in the tomb, the world fabricates a false illusion of "life"

Deep from inside its tomb of death, indifference, and oppression, the world pretends to give the appearance of life. In order to do so, the world portrays death as life, injustice as a normal state of collective life, oppression as a necessary condition for human existence, indifference as a necessary sedative to bring tranquility, and lies as a means to obscure the truth.

There is one way for us to get out of the tomb: by participating in the life and unity of the trinitarian God! We can be united to the risen

Jesus by continuing the works he did while on earth, by *"doing good and healing all those oppressed by the devil"* (*Acts* 10:38). That is to say, by liberating the victims of all types of evil, individual and collective.

He who participates in the life of the communitarian God can say, *"I shall not die but live and declare the deeds of the Lord"* (*Psalm* 118:17).

3. The restoration of communitarian life is like a new dawn

In the dawn of creation, the light was with man, inasmuch as he had been created in the image of a communitarian God. Man was free to grow in the goodness he had received; he lived in the peace and unity of the human community in accordance with God's design. However, unity was fragmented when men disobeyed the will of God, divided themselves into antagonistic groups, and sought their mutual destruction. By so harming their own human dignity, men sank humanity into darkness.

The light of dawn (the resurrection) reappears when God, through Jesus Christ, removes the stone of the tomb of division and subjugation in order for men to come out of the darkness into the light and to return to communitarian life. This is the second and never-ending dawn of humanity.

Men *run to see this wonder* (*John* 20:1-9). They cannot rest until they see the stone removed; they rejoice at seeing the end of divisions and subjugation, the end of the exploitation of man by man, and the end of all wars. They will continue to run toward their new life with the excitement that fills those who run toward unity and liberation, those who move from darkness to light, and from night to dawn. Even to this day, it is everyone's responsibility to see to it that the stone is removed.

The stone of the tomb is the burden that overwhelms us when we live amidst antagonistic individuals, groups, and nations. With the triumph of unitarian life, we fully restore our human dignity and enter into the second dawn of humanity – a renewal of the first dawn when God created man in his own image and likeness.

The restoration of the human community follows a process

These are the phases of this process:

A. Human life began in the image of God. From the beginning, God bestowed his image and likeness upon men. We were truly alive, for we were the image of God and participated in the order intended by him as his children living in the fullness of unity and equality. This is a life of *"sincerity and truth"* (*1 Corinthians* 5:8).

B. Then came the phase of division and oppression imposed by man upon man, causing the destruction of the unity and equality among them. This was the state of *"malice and wickedness"* (*1 Corinthians* 5:8) that drove us away from our initial state of life. It was a grave step backward in the evolution of humanity.

C. Finally, God intervened. He came into a world alienated by *malice and wickedness*, injustice and oppression ominously imposed upon men. It was this world of *malice and wickedness* that perverted communitarian life in the world. Through the resurrection of Jesus Christ, however, God defeated the world of death and restored man to his initial life. Christ restored the life of *sincerity and truth* among human beings. The resurrection is, therefore, the greatest evolutionary leap forward for humanity.

With life reinstated, we regained our ability to live to the fullest again; we retook what we had lost to malice and wickedness, to injustice, division, and oppression. Life had been restored to the initial state intended by God. The completion of the process of resurrection occurs when all human beings come to share in the life of the communitarian God.

Chapter VIII

THE COMMUNITARIAN ECONOMY AND THE COMMUNITARIAN LEADERS

1. Characteristics of a communitarian economy

*W*hen men live in community, they, necessarily, promote an economic community from which no one is excluded, in which God is present in the midst of all men: *"All who believed were together and had all things in common; they would sell their property and possessions and divide them among all according to each one's need"* (*Acts* 2:44-45).

In this human community, all men live in unity with one another and in unity with God through *the breaking of the bread and prayers* (*Acts* 2:42). In this community prevails the common good over individual interests, and mutual respect over domination. In this community, all goods are held in common, and are a source of unity among its members

Even more, communal life goes beyond economics, as it encompasses other aspects of human life, such as:

– Unity of faith, whereby all members share one conviction, one belief.
– Unity of action, whereby everybody shares the wealth in common.

— Unity of hope, whereby all share one goal, which is the wellbeing of all – without exception.

A communitarian economy is, therefore, a sign of God's presence in our midst, is a sign of the presence of the risen Christ among us. However, by rejecting communal life, the world rejects the resurrection because the existence of antagonistic groups and nations is in direct opposition to the unity, peace, harmony, and mutual understanding, which are proper to communal life and resurrection. Conversely, by restoring common unity in human life, both individually and collectively, we begin to possess the life of the resurrection here on earth.

**Human unity requires an economic system
at the service of humanity**

What is an economic system? It is the organized manner in which a given society arranges and manages the production, distribution, and consumption of goods in order to meet the needs of its members. The fundamental purpose of an economic system is to ensure that all men, without exception, participate in the production, distribution, and consumption of economic goods.

The fact that a few individuals take possession of the wealth, while the vast majorities live in poverty, is an indication that the world's economic systems have failed to live up to their responsibility and purpose. An economic system that fails to meet the needs of all is a "dead" economic system and, therefore, needs to be "brought back to life." Again, an economy that provides for the wellbeing of everyone is the only economic system that can fully serve the needs of humankind; the only economic system fit for a life of resurrection.

2. Those who take upon themselves the task of changing an unjust socioeconomic system may experience fears

The monumental task of changing an unjust socioeconomic system into a just one may, to some extent, be the cause of serious fears in those who are supposed to undertake such a task. These fears can be similar to those experienced by the disciples of Jesus when, after his resurrection, *"he stood in their midst and said to them, 'Peace be with you'. But they were startled and terrified and thought they were seeing a ghost" (Luke 24: 36-37).* The following are the fears:

- Fear of failure. It sets in whenever a person fails to live up to the expectations that he has set for himself or others have set for him. When men pledge loyalty to God and are unable to live up to it, then they become frightened at the prospect of having to render an account of their disloyalty; they are afraid of finding themselves in the presence of the risen Lord who has defeated death.
- Fear of an impending harm. If a leader is put to death, then his followers may become frightened at the prospect that they may also be put to death.
- Fear of losing a loved one forever. Whoever loses a loved one to death, undergoes the fear of being abandoned because death is an irreparable loss and nobody comes back from it.
- Fear of the unknown. It is the fear of darkness, of uncertainty, of not knowing what or who comes next.
- Fear of oneself. After having lost someone who was an integral part of us, we may come to the realization that we have been left incomplete as persons.

Those fears could be devastating since living in fear is like not living at all.

The presence of Christ brings an end to our fears

Whatever our fears may be, Christ is always before us, reminding us that he is truly alive, truly caring, truly loving. No matter how much division, destruction and oppression we may experience in this world, it is up to us to see that Christ is with us, dispelling our fears and aiding us in the restoration of the unity, peace and justice proper to the human community.

God is present in the human community

The life of Christ in the world is not just a historical event, it is a real presence in all men. By his presence, he frees men from the limitations of time and space as well as from the structures of oppression and injustice. Through his presence, God allows men to project themselves onto the future in the continuity of generations. Without such presence, men would succumb to the destructive forces of antagonistic societies. Through his presence in men, God reasserts himself as the author of history, filling it with his spirit so the actions of men, throughout history, become a true expression of their life in freedom and unity.

By virtue of God's presence in us, those who hold worldly power are no longer the usurpers of history. They lose their power to distort history, they no longer can justify, as necessary events of history, the injustice they inflict upon their fellow human beings.

To those who live in a human community, the life of Christ is not just the temporal passing of historical events, of *"things that happened to Jesus the Nazarene, who was a prophet mighty in deed and word . . . [who was] handed over to a sentence of death"* (*Luke* 24:19-20). Rather, the life of Christ in men, gives continuity to their human community beyond the limitations of historical events.

It is a historic reality that life in the human community undergoes times of crises and trials but its members take upon themselves the responsibility of restoring their unity in compliance of their communitarian nature. If that were not the case, we would have to conclude that men are destined to never overcome class antagonisms, and that the human community is just an illusion. Therefore, to affirm: *"we were hoping that he would be the one to redeem [our people]"* (*Luke* 24:21) is the equivalent to deny the presence of God in us, in the present moment, and beyond the historical events.

Christ is beyond history and beyond the forces of those who institute division, conflict and antagonism among the peoples of the world. By his presence in the world, Christ demonstrates that the dominant powers of society can no longer dictate the meaning and course of history. By his presence in us, the Redeemer allows us to take over our destiny in truth and in freedom. The life of Christ in history only has meaning when we see it as a presence leading us along the way to unity and peace in this world and to his eternal presence (*Luke* 24:27).

3. The leaders in the human community

He is a true communitarian leader who possesses the following attributes:

- A true leader's life is based on unity and equality.
- A true leader values unity as a treasure that enriches the entire human race.
- A true leader makes a commitment to share his life with all. The force that moves him is the desire to bring unity to everybody. His leadership, therefore, is based on his identification with his followers.
- A true leader leads through example in favorable times and in times of challenges. He becomes a gift to all who follow him. He draws his fallowers to him, and becomes one with them arriving together at the common goal of human community

On the contrary, the leaders of class societies fail to meet the requirements of true leadership:

- They lack life within themselves because there is no life in those, whose only concern is the acquisition of wealth and power at all cost.
- They are committed only to making a "better" life for themselves, disregarding the welfare of others.
- They build an insurmountable wall of separation between themselves and those whom they are supposed to lead.

The leaders of class societies are thieves and robbers who come *"only to steal and slaughter and destroy"* (*John* 10:10); they are the ones who do *"not enter… through the gate but climb over elsewhere"* (*John* 10:1).

It is worth repeating that a communitarian leader brings unity to the people so that they, together, may *"have life and have it more abundantly"* (*John* 10:10).

Why do men refuse to live in unity? For the following reasons:

A. Because class societies have instituted inequality as the foundation of the relations between their members: superiors and inferiors, rulers and subjects, the powerful and the weak, the oppressor and the oppressed.

B. Because those who exert dominion lack the capacity to follow the communitarian model. How could it be possible that those who seek their own interests would willingly decide to eradicate the divisions between superior and inferior, ruler and subject?

In his gospel, John describes the leaders of a class society as "*the hire men*" who have "*no concern for the sheep*" (*John* 10: 12,13); they are only concerned with their welfare, and disregard the welfare of others.

The good shepherd (Jesus Christ) is the model to be followed by the communitarian leaders because "*a good shepherd lays down his life for the sheep*" (*John* 10:11). The relationship between the good shepherd and the flock is not so much that of a leader and his followers, but rather that of a person who gives his own life for the benefit of those for whom he cares.

The good shepherd freely lays down his life for those he loves, and he loves everyone. Why does he love them? Because they are sons and daughters of God, just as Christ himself is the Son of God. By giving his life for us, the good shepherd opens the way for us to "*be like him*" (*1 John* 3:2), to join him as members of the community of men and God. However, "the good shepherd" continues to be rejected by a world whereby division, inequality, and exploitation are the norm.

4. The way leading to life and the way leading to God are one and the same

As a good shepherd, Jesus Christ leads us to the fulfillment of our human nature, the fulfillment of who we truly are, the fulfillment of our communitarian life. Those who follow Jesus become more than just his followers, they become one with the shepherd inasmuch as he is the way and the life: "*My sheep hear my voice; I know them, and they follow me. I give them eternal life, and they shall never perish"* (*John* 10: 27, 28). It is by following the path of Christ that we are on our way to achieve eternal life starting here on earth.

"The Lamb who is in the center of the throne will shepherd them and lead them to springs of life-giving water, and God will wipe away every tear from their eyes" (*Revelation* 7:17).

The world does not know the way that leads to life. Why?

- Because the world refuses to know how a person becomes one with God. Our world rejects the unity between men and God and between men themselves. The world knows, however, how to divide mankind into antagonistic nations and groups.
- Because the world refuses to follow the way that leads to communitarian life. The world follows the way that leads to domination and to wealth for only a few. The world follows the way that leads to the alienation of human dignity by turning people into tools to achieve the selfish interests of the dominant classes.
- Because the world persecutes those who promote the path to *common unity*: *"The leading [people] of the city stirred up a persecution against Paul and Barnabas and expelled them from their territory"* (*Acts* 13:50).

The beginning and end of persecution:

- A persecution begins as a means used by the powerful in order to destroy those who seek equality and unity.
- A persecution comes to and end with the final triumph of those who fight for unity and equality. They *"are the ones who have survived the time of great distress [persecution]; they have washed their robes and made them white in the blood of the Lamb"* (*Revelation* 7:14).

Through his resurrection, Christ draws the human community into the community of the trinitarian God. In other words, resurrection is the restoration of eternal life in our human life, and the convergence of our earthly life and our heavenly life. This is so because Christ himself is alive both in heaven and on earth (not just in heaven): *"Look at my hands and my feet, that it is I myself. Touch me and see me, because a ghost does not have flesh and bones, as you can see, I have"* (*Luke* 24:39). Furthermore, if God is alive in us, it necessarily follows that we are alive in him.

To deny that Christ lives both on earth and in heaven is the equivalent of saying that he does not live at all. To some people, God is not alive at all because his presence represents a constant obstacle to those who promote inequalities and antagonisms in the world. Those who deny that Christ is alive do it in two ways: by their actions and by their omissions.

- By their actions, that is, by the injustices and abuses they commit, which places them in radical opposition to the God of unity and peace. They are the ones *who put to death the author of life* (*Acts* 3:15).
- By their omissions, that is, by their refusal to restore unity and equality among human beings. Another form of omission consists in *"seeing"* only certain forms of evil while remaining totally blind to other grave offenses against justice and human dignity.

Once we see that Christ is alive, both on earth and in heaven, we will be able to see that our own life is the convergence of our earthly life with our heavenly life.

The advance towards the restoration of the human community may be hindered by regressions

Regression is an evasion of our responsibility to move forward towards our individual and collective wellbeing; it is a disservice to ourselves and to our fellow human beings. Frequently, men are prone to forget even the goodness they have learned and experienced along their lives; they are prone to return to their old ways of life. *"Simon Peter said to [the other disciples], 'I am going fishing.' They said to him, 'We also will come with you'"* (*John* 21:3).

By their regression, men hinder human progress; for if they refuse to make God's life of unity grow in the world, who will lead humanity toward progress, who will engaged in the work of God? If no one is to do the work of God, there will be no leap from death to life, from division to unity, from injustice to justice. In summary, there will be no liberation for humanity.

Regression is tantamount to denying God

Those who live in God are always moving forward towards common unity among the peoples of the world. Nevertheless, when men are intent on regressing, God intervenes to move them forward, to give them courage to remain faithful to the work that leads humanity to fullness of life in community. Otherwise, regression will cause the eventual annihilation of humanity. ¿Who would be satisfied living in a world moving backwards to the tomb of mutual destruction?

Chapter IX

THE LOVE BETWEEN GOD AND MEN LEADS TO UNITY

From the time of their appearance on earth, men lived in unity among themselves and in unity with God, until the time they established antagonistic groups and began destroying one another. Their continued mutual destruction meant that men not only separated themselves from God, but also became reluctant to take the way that leads back to him.

Christ Jesus came to the world to lead us all back to the Father, so that *"where [he is, we] also may be"* (*John* 14:3).

Since the inception of antagonistic groups, men have systematically refused to follow the way that leads to God. However, their rejection of the God made-man is based, not so much in their refusal to accept God, but in their refusal to accept man.

People do not accept that a man can possess God's nature because our world exploits men; thus, it becomes unacceptable that he, who is subject to exploitation, may even remotely share in the divine nature, let alone be the Way to God.

The reason for Christ to come to the world was to restore men to their lost dignity of being the image and likeness of the Creator, to restore their ability to live in unity, and to free them from mutual destruction.

This is how we return to God:

- By seeing him in every person.
- By doing his works.
- By restoring our ability to live in unity and equality among ourselves.
- By accepting that God unifies his divine nature with our human nature.

The following is an example of how to take the way that leads to God: when *"the Hellenist complained against the Hebrews ... the Twelve called together the community ... [proposed a solution, and] the proposal was acceptable to the whole community"* (*Acts* 6:1-5). The peaceful, honest, and rational approach to resolving human conflicts is one of the ways that leads us to God. Conversely, resorting to intolerance leads to the perpetuation of conflicts and absence of unity.

1. Human life is nurtured by divine life

Just as the life of the branches comes from the vine, the life of men comes from God. No one, individually or collectively, can live unless he draws his life from God. This is how a human society takes its life from God:

- A society where people do not destroy each other is alive because it partakes in the life of the communitarian God.
- A society that respects equality among its members is alive because it partakes in the equality of the Persons of the Trinity (Father, Son and Holy Spirit).
- A society whose members live in unity is alive because it follows the example of the Redeemer, who made himself one with humanity.
- A society wherein everyone is treated as being the image of the Creator is alive because it follows his truth.

The life that comes from God is true life because it makes us who we are, it allows us to continue living on this earth, and it will take us onto eternity if we remain faithful to it. When human societies are filled with that life, they become the *"branches" that "will live for the Lord" (Psalm* 22:31), that will *"bear much fruit" (John* 15:8).

In order to remain in the vine, we must *"love not in word or speech but in deed and truth" (1 John* 3:18). Since the Lord is freedom, we must live in freedom; since the Lord is love, we must love one another. Anyone who does not remain in the vine, that is, in God, will be *"thrown out like a branch and wither" (John* 15:6). But if we remain in the vine, we will *"ask for whatever [we] want and it will be done for [us]" (John* 15:7); for what belongs to the vine, also belongs to the branches.

Love is the unifying bond which makes us human

"This is how all will know that you are my disciples, if you have love for one another" (John 13:35).

Human beings reveal who they truly are by their love for one another. Therefore, this love cannot be compromised under any circumstances. When there is no love, there is no human person; that is, the absence of love takes away the humanness in a person.

What is this love? How do we define it?
How do we come to know it?

This love is the bond that unites the totality of a person with another person and with the entire humanity. Consequently, if this love involves the totality of a person, it means that it is not just a mere sentiment or a feeling or an emotion or a passion, which connects one person with others. Rather it involves one's whole being in a total unity with others.

Those who love with total love are the ones who reveal themselves as true human persons before the eyes of God and the world.

Christian love comes from the Almighty and is disseminated among humans

The unifying love which makes us humans would not be possible if God himself had not demonstrated to us that his trinitarian love is truly unifying. It is often said that men comply with the commandment of love in the same way a subordinate obeys an order from his commander just as if God were imposing an obligation among his followers. In order to refute this notion, we can say that whenever God gives a commandment, he also gives his life with it. In other words, he loves by giving his life for those whom he loves. Christian love means that giving a commandment involves not only the giving of an order but, above all, it involves the giving of oneself, the giving of one's life.

Jesus lives in us because through his commandments, he gives us his life. He tells us, *"You are in me and I in you"* (*John* 14:20); *"I live and you will live"* (*John* 14:19). Through his commandments, Christ Jesus gives us his life, and by keeping his commandments, we live in him and become one with him, and with all the members of the human race as well.

How do we disseminate the life we receive from God?

- By seeking the welfare of all, not so much because we are compelled to do so by an external commandment, but because our life is united to the life of all our fellow human beings – what is ours, is also theirs.
- By seeking the welfare, not only of those who think or behave like us, but those who think and behave differently than us. That is, those who might be, or are our enemies. The life we receive from the Almighty is, necessarily, for all humans on account of his commandment of universal unity.

The Spirit of God – *"the Spirit of truth"* – comes to live in those who keep his commandments. However, *"the world cannot accept the Spirit of truth, because it neither sees nor knows it"* (*John* 14:17).

Those who live under the mentality of the world do not see or know the Spirit of Truth because they are concerned only with their own selfish interests (or those of their group or their nation). They do not establish unity with those whom they rule over; on the contrary, they create an ever-widening gap between themselves and their citizenry. Under these circumstances, it is not possible to establish a community of life between those who give the law and those who receive it.

Again, when God gives a commandment, he gives himself with it, establishing an unbreakable unity of life with the recipients. Thus, the Lord's commandments are impregnated with his own life, and whoever receives them assumes the responsibility to pass them along to other human beings in the same manner.

2. The love between God and man is a necessity

The love between God and man is, above all, a necessity, the necessity of a person to be the image and likeness of his Creator, the necessity to live as a human being expressing the trinitarian unity that exists in his humanness. Love is a necessity because men need to live in accordance with the truth and unity, which are in God, or else humanity will destroy itself. Love is the means to preserve the integrity of humankind.

There are two requirements to love:

- We must begin by renouncing all forms of harming one another. Our world must strive at meeting this minimum requisite. For it is evident that nowadays, in our world, men destroy one another in so many ways – as individuals and as nations.
- We must promote equality and unity among all, even at the cost of one's own life. For this is what the Son of God did in order to demonstrate his love for us.

Peace is the fruit of love

While the trinitarian God reveals that love engenders peace, the world, divided into antagonistic classes, finds itself in need of establishing its own definition of peace. In the gospel of John, Jesus defines the difference between the peace of God and the peace of the world: *"Peace I leave with you; my peace I give to you. Not as the world gives do I give it to you"* (*John* 14:27).

The peace Christ gives differs radically from the peace the world gives.

A. The peace Christ gives is the product of us having freely allowed him to make his dwelling in us. In other words, it is because we allow Christ to dwell in us that he gives us the only genuine peace – the peace that comes from our own willingness, not from external coercion.

The peace Christ gives frees us from cowardice and fear in the face of persecution and struggle: *"Do not let your hearts be troubled or afraid"* (*John* 14:27). The one who seeks the peace of Christ will be under relentless opposition from the enemies of peace, and yet he will never lose heart.

B. The peace the world gives is the product of an imposition. It is a form of control imposed by a power group for the sole purpose of maintaining an "established order" that will ensure the submission of the subjects. Therefore, the peace the world gives is no peace at all, and only makes God's peace all the more urgent.

The peace the world gives generates fear both in the one who receives it and in the one who gives it:

- Fear in the one who receives it. The peace the world gives is imposed by coercion and threats of impending harm, which create fear in those who receive it and in those who attempt to free themselves from such "peace."
- Fear in the one who gives it. He who gives the peace of the world will live in fear of retaliation and will be possessed by a sense of insecurity, not knowing when and how the victims of the peace of the world will react.

The dominant socioeconomic classes condone, for their own convenience, the peace the world gives, and promote it by spreading the false conception that there is no other way to live in "peace." To such classes, the peace of God is nothing but a mere illusion, which will never become a reality.

3. The love of God leads us to eternal life

Anyone who aspires to eternal life must first have life here on earth. Therefore, here on earth, we need to have the life that is in God and has been since *"before the world began"* (*John* 17:5). We need to have the very life of God who has *"authority over all people so that he may give eternal life to all"* (*John* 17:2).

A confrontation develops

The one who brings life to the world will find he is in opposition to a world immersed in a culture of death. There is a time when that confrontation comes to a head: *"Father the hour has come"* (*John* 17:1), the hour when the world displays its power. The power it uses so well: death.

And so it happens that the one who brings life is killed, only to rise from the dead and restore the imperishable unifying life that comes from the Almighty. God glorifies those who restore life with the glory that has been in him since *"before the world began"* (*John* 17:1, 5).

How do we become one with God? *"By accomplishing the work that [God gives us] to do"* (*John* 17:4). That is to say, by forgiving our enemies, by blessing those who curse us, by doing good to those who do us wrong, by freeing the oppressed, and by taking care of the ill. No one who is in sincere pursuit of becoming one with God can exclude himself from doing the works the Son of God did when he walked this world.

Divine life is a visualization of God

In order to see God, all a person needs to do is look at his fellow human beings. Consequently, any harm we may cause others is an indication that we are unable to *see* the image and likeness of God in them, for if we were able to see God in them, we would not harm them. Furthermore, he who offends others offends himself because we all share in the same image and likeness.

A way for men to avoid seeing God in their fellowmen is through isolationism, which shields them from seeing the harm they cause their victims. The failure of a person (or a nation) to see God in others produces in him two effects:

A. He lives without God; that is, he excludes him from his life.

B. He replaces God with something else: he makes his own gods – the god of wealth, of power, of prestige, of indifference, and so forth.

Why is God in our fellow human beings?

Because he relates to us through other human beings. And this is the way God, in Christ, relates to us: he makes himself one of us. Therefore, when we love our neighbors, we love the God who is in them. To know that Christ loves us is to know that he is in us: *"We have come to know and believe in the love of God for us"* (*1 John* 4:16). Thus, we see God, not so much ***through*** our fellow human beings, but rather ***in*** them.

4. To love God means to be one with him

"May all be one, as you, Father, are in me and I in you, . . . I in them and you in me, that they may be brought to perfection as one" (*John* 17:21, 23).

Living in unity means that a person lives **in** another, not **with** another. When I say, "you live in me" I am making you an integral and essential part of me; that is to say, I do not live unless you live in me.

The unity among men, therefore, is not a mere conglomeration of bodies placed in close proximity to each other, but rather, it is the sharing of the totality of their spirits – that is, their ideals, feelings, aspirations, emotions, etc. It is obvious that living in another does not refer to the body (which would be an impossibility), but to the spirit.

The world does not see unity in this manner, or understand it because this unity involves the elements of human nature over which the powers of the world have no dominion.

True unity maintains the integrity of humanity for, how could I dare destroy my brother if by virtue of him living in me, he is an essential part of me? If we were to live this kind of unity, men would never harm or destroy one another. But they do, this is why humanity must turn to true unity.

Unity understood as the presence of a person in another person is what makes life immortal, inasmuch as the person who dies continues to live in those who come after him. Without living in one another we are nothing but a bunch of bodies huddled one next to the other. Let us present a simple but graphic example: in the game of football, the players huddle next to each other in order to unify their thoughts regarding their next play as a team.

Unity as the presence of a person in another can be applied to the unity between man and God (*John* 17:21-23). In a state of unity, man and God share their whole beings, their ideals, their thoughts, and their love. God invites us to participate in this kind of unity with him and with every human being as well.

The opposite of unity among men is division, which is brought about by indifference and destruction.

- Indifference is the equivalent of saying to another, "you do not exist." Which is a dangerous statement meaning, if you do not exist, neither do I.
- Destruction is the equivalent of saying: "I will bring an end to your existence." Which is another dangerous statement meaning if I destroy you, I destroy myself in the process.

Chapter X

HUMAN LABOR AS A FOUNT
OF COMMUNITARIAN LIFE

$\mathcal{S}$ince the beginning of human life on earth, the Creator's plan was for men to be the protagonists of their own evolution by exercising their innate freedom. Throughout hundreds of thousands of years, men were able to live in unity and equality among themselves, and in harmony with their environment. Had it been otherwise, men would have destroyed themselves, even in the initial stages of their evolution. There came, however, a moment in history when man misused his freedom (a disobedience to the plan of God), causing the breakage of unity and the establishment of a state of injustice (a *state of sin*). From thereon, the history of mankind has been an ongoing struggle between those who seek the restoration of the human community and those who persist on maintaining the *status quo*.

The event that signals the beginning of the end to the state of injustice and sin is the coming of God to the world as a man: *"Behold the Lamb of God, who takes away the sin of the world"* (*John* 1:29).

Christ comes to take away the sin of the world, and to reinstate the unity that exists in him even before men ever existed. As Christ comes to the world, he continues to rank ahead of us because he existed before us. John the Baptist says: *"A man is coming after me who ranks ahead of* *me because he existed before me"* (*John* 1:30). Our historical responsibility, therefore, is to make God's liberation a reality in the world, to work with him in restoring our human unity, and to bring an end to the state of sin.

With the coming of Christ to the world, men retake their responsibility to turn their human labor into a source of unification and a means to eradicate all forms of division. Insofar as only men can reunify men, God made himself a man and continues to seek other men willing to join him in the work of unifying humankind.

1. Fishers of men and the followers of Christ

Christ seeks *"fishers of men"* (*Matthew* 4: 19) because only men can bring unity to themselves, and there is nothing in the universe of greater value than men. So great is their value that God tells them: *"the Kingdom of heaven is at hand"* (*Matthew* 4:17).

Who are the fishers of men? They are those who join Christ in the work of bringing about unity to all, and liberation from all forms of conflicts and antagonisms. Therefore, a fisher of men must see men as God sees them, namely:

A. A fisher of men acknowledges the supremacy of a human being over everything else in the universe, for only a human being is *the image of God.*

B. A fisher of men fully understands the need to rescue men whenever they lose such supremacy. A fisher of men is the *"great light"* which shines *"on those dwelling in a land overshadowed by death"* (*Matthew* 4:16).

How do men lose their unity?

Men lose their unity whenever they exploit one another and whenever they treat each other as if they were unequal. In other words, the loss of human unity is the manifestation of men's failure to live as humans.

The loss of unity affects both the perpetrators and their victims. The perpetrators are affected because they fail to treat people in accordance with their human dignity, and the victims, because they are forcefully deprived of it.

How do men restore their unity?

Men restore their unity by ensuring that *"there be no divisions among [them], but that [they] be united in the same mind and in the same purpose"* (*1 Corinthians* 1:10).

Fishers of men have the task of ensuring that people do live as equals and in unity so the work of God *"might not be emptied of its meaning"* (*1 Corinthians* 1:17). In other words, we share in God's work whenever we restore our unity. Fishers of men not only work *with* God or *for* God, but essentially, work *in* God, and are part of God. They go about the world *"proclaiming the gospel of the Kingdom, and curing every disease and illness among the people"* (*Matthew* 4:23), especially the illnesses afflicting the unity among the member of humankind.

By restoring unity and equality, a fisher of men smashes *"the yoke that burdened [the people], the pole on their shoulder and the rod of their taskmaster"* (*Isaiah* 9:3). This work is, basically, one of liberation.

Recommendations to return to communitarian life

Practicing the beatitudes is the surest way to return to communitarian life because they are the means to merge human life with the life of the trinitarian God, they set the foundations of heaven here on earth. Through them, men establish a continuity of earthly life and heavenly life.

Who are they who practice the beatitudes? (*Matthew* 5:1-11)

- *The poor in spirit* are those whose confidence is in God (not in material possessions), they utilize material possessions exclusively for the common good.
- *Those who mourn* are the ones capable of joining in the suffering of the oppressed; they have the sensitivity to identify themselves with the oppressed.

- *The meek* are the ones who are sincere and honest in their relations with others, as opposed to being deceitful, arrogant, false and dishonest; they restore truth and trust to the relations between people.
- *Those who hunger and thirst for righteousness* are the ones who can lead humankind to liberation and keep the course toward justice and common unity.
- *The merciful* bring compassionate justice (as opposed to vengeance) to all.
- *The clean of heart* are the ones who understand and pursue the wellbeing of everybody (as opposed to pursuing their own selfish interests); they do not mean ill to, or take advantage of anyone.
- *The peacemakers* are the ones who see in every person a brother or sister because we are all children of God. The peacemakers do not destroy, they edify.
- *Those who are persecuted for the sake of righteousness* are the ones who do not compromise with injustice and oppression, they do not settle for anything less than the total restoration of the human community, and have begun to build the kingdom of heaven here and now.

The beatitudes always enhance life

Those who live the beatitudes enhance their own life and that of their fellow human beings with the life of God who is constantly and incessantly acting in and through them, intervening in human history.

This is how to live the beatitudes: *by securing justice for the oppressed, feeding the hungry, setting prisoners free, giving sight to the blind, raising up those who are bowed down, loving the righteous, protecting the stranger, sustaining the orphan and the widow, and thwarting the way of the wicked* (*Psalm* 146:7-9).

The beatitudes will overcome the standards of the world

Those who embrace the beatitudes will overcome the world's standards because *"God chose the foolish of the world to shame the wise, and*

God chose the weak of the world to shame the strong, and God chose the lowly and despised of the world, those who count for nothing, to reduce to nothing those who are something" (*1 Corinthians* 1:27-28).

The one who practices the beatitudes assumes the role of a leader

By practicing the beatitudes, Christ Jesus become the model for every person, and the *"Lamb of God"* for all humankind. To said that the "Lamb" is a leader may seem, at first sight, contradictory but the Lamb of God, however, proves there is no such contradiction.

"Behold, the Lamb of God" (*John* 1:36), behold the one who takes upon himself God's will, in order to make our old world new, to bring divisions to and end and restore justice and unity at the cost of sacrificing his own life (as a *sacrificial lamb*). This is the true leader worthy of following.

Now, when we decide to follow Christ, he will ask us: *"What are you looking for?"* (*John* 1:38). If indeed we are looking for him, we may want to know whether he has the means to give us what we are looking for; consequently, we ask him: *"Where are you staying?"* Then, in order that there may be no doubt as to what he stands for, Christ replies: *"Come, and you will see"* (*John* 1:39).

Christ Jesus has nothing to hide. He reveals his very self to all who want to join him. He shares with us all he is and all he has; he becomes one with those who join him: *"whoever is joined to the Lord becomes one in spirit with him"* (*1 Corinthians* 6:17). Just as a man becomes one with God, so does every institution of human society, inasmuch as an institution is a collectivity of men. Thus, the Lamb of God leads the individual and humankind towards a world of common unity.

2. "The world in its present form is passing away"

"The world in its present form is passing away" (*1 Corinthians* 7:31). And, what is the world's "present form"? It is a world divided into antagonistic classes, without unity and equality, a world where the powerful appropriate for themselves what the workers produce, a world where people exploit and destroy one another.

With the arrival of *"the time of fulfillment"* and with *"the Kingdom of God at hand"* (*Mark* 1:15), we must assume our responsibility to transform the world's present form into a world of unity and equality, a world that embraces justice and peace. In order to bring an end to the world in its present form and to build a new world, Christ recruits *"fishers of men"* (*Mark* 1:17)

The following are the transformations needed to turn *the world in its present* into a new world:

- The transformation of those who administer the wealth of the world. They can transform themselves into *fishers of men* by establishing socioeconomic systems that allow all men to produce and enjoy the fruits of their labor.
- The transformation of those who run the political institutions of the world. They can transform themselves into *fishers of men* by governing in order to fulfill the common good.
- The transformation of those who are responsible for the spiritual life of the people. They can transform themselves into *fishers of men* by addressing men as whole persons made of body and soul, not just soul.

These transformations are necessary because *this is the time of fulfillment and the Kingdom of God is at hand.*

The restoration of the human community requires corrective actions

Mark in his gospel presents a situation where Jesus liberates a man from an unclean spirit. *"In their synagogue was a man with an unclean spirit; he cried out, 'What have you to do with us, Jesus of Nazareth? Have you come to destroy us?'... Jesus rebuked him and said, 'Quiet! Come out of him!' The unclean spirit convulsed him and with a loud cry came out of him"* (*Mark* 1:23-26).

Just as Christ expels the unclean spirit from a man, so he will expel all evils from our world – injustice, exploitation of man by man, mutual destruction –; and just as the possessed man went into "convulsions" before the evil spirit left him, so will the world undergo violent convulsions before it is freed from all forms of evil.

Evil infiltrates all spheres of human society

Evil can infiltrate our families, our societal institutions under seemingly "acceptable" forms, and hide in them. But the presence of God forces evil to come out from hiding.

Evil cannot hide from God

People who pursue truth and goodness have the power to expose evil. God's presence in us gives us the ability to identify, expose, and expel evil wherever evil is found, for good and evil cannot coexist with each other, and the struggle between the two produces *violent convulsions*.

God's authority to expel the evils hidden in our society is radically different from the authority of those who speak in the name of their own gods: the gods of earthly power. God warns us that if a person *"presumes to speak in my name a word that I have not commanded him to speak, or speaks in the name of other gods, he shall die"* (*Deuteronomy* 18:20).

3. The restoration of communitarian life brings about the common good

Whenever men are divided into antagonistic socioeconomic classes, the powerful appropriate for themselves the wealth produced by the working classes, thus, creating profound gaps of inequality: scandalous wealth, on the side of the rich, and inhuman misery on the side of the poor. Inequality and injustice, however, will be eliminated through the restoration of the human community, with men resorting to mutual cooperation in the production of economic goods and to justice in the distribution of the wealth produced. Otherwise, inequalities, injustice, and exploitation will become endemic.

Levels of poverty within an unjust society

A. At the individual level, there is economic poverty, which consists in the lack of means for survival; there is poverty of compassion, which consists in the lack of interest in alleviating the sufferings of our fellow human beings; there is poverty of hope in a better world; there is poverty of faith in ourselves and in God.

B. At the collective level, we are running out of justice, equality, peace and respect among nations. The world is being torn apart by strife, aggression, predatory wars, and economic policies that produce hunger and starvation all over the world. In short, we are running out of life.

How to restore social wellbeing for everybody

A. By identifying and denouncing all forms of poverty in us as individuals and as a world community.

B. By turning our human potentials into ways to achieve equality, justice, peace, mutual respect, cooperation, and understanding among individuals and nations.

A society without the capacity to attend to the needs of its members is like a wedding party running out of wine. We need to present to God our human potentials and our material resources and he will help us transform our scarcities into abundance for all to "drink", just as Christ, at Cana, transformed simple water into the best wine (*John* 2:9).

4. A job assigned to everybody

This is how Jesus Christ took over the job the Father assigned to him: *"The spirit of the Lord is upon me, because he has anointed me to bring glad tidings to the poor. He has sent me to proclaim liberty to captives and recovery of sight to the blind, to let the oppressed go free, and to proclaim a year acceptable to the Lord"* (*Luke* 4:18-19).

Now, we all have been assigned the same job, and it is our responsibility to get it done: *"the assembly, which consisted of men, women, and those children old enough to understand . . . their hands raised high, answered, 'Amen, amen'"* (*Nehemiah* 8:2,6). The people hear God's voice and respond to it by making it part of their life.

The world tries to prevent us from taking over our assignment

A struggle ensues between those who are ready to undertake the job of restoring unity among men and a world satisfied with maintaining the status quo. In this struggle, the more the world tries to prevent us from fulfilling our assignment, the stronger our determination grows:

- The more inequality the world creates, the greater is the need for us to restore equality.
- The more injustice is inflicted upon mankind, the greater is the need for us to restore justice.
- The more oppression is forced upon us, the more we need to bring about liberation.
- The more the world resorts to wars and destruction, the more we struggle for peace and mutual respect.
- The more the world offends human dignity, the more we struggle to restore the dignity of every person.
- The more the world tries to keep us in the darkness of ignorance, submission, indifference, complaisance, and egotism, the more we look for the light that leads to fullness of life in the human community.

The scope of the assignment

The job of restoring the human community is not assigned just to one nation, or one group; it is assigned to all humankind, *"so that there may be no division in the body, but that the parts may have the same concern for one another"* (*1 Corinthians* 12:25).

God made himself a man, in Christ Jesus, so that we may join him in the work of restoring the human community and the common good

Now, the logical question is the following: why do men reject the God who made himself man? Precisely, because God made himself a man... a man of the lower strata of human society, without riches, with no earthly power; a man who was as much despised as anybody else among the despised. *"The people in the synagogue... were all filled with fury. They rose up, drove him [Jesus] out of the town, and led him to the brow of the hill on which their town had been built, to hurl him down headlong"* (*Luke* 4:28-29). It is extremely difficult for the powerful of the world to accept a God who made himself a poor and powerless man... a man who, pretty much, had nothing in common with the powerful.

But, why even the powerless reject the God made man? Because they are under the control and influence of the dominant classes. And, the powerful, through their laws and institutions, have the means to mold the minds and control the actions of the oppressed.

Upon coming into the world, God introduces himself as one of us – *"Isn't this the son of Joseph?"* (*Luke* 4:22) –, a member of a human family in order to demonstrate that the dignity of his human family is as real as the dignity of his divine family. He introduces himself as someone whose family is composed of the great and the lowly, the poor and the wealthy, the ill and the healthy, the born and the unborn, the faithful and the unfaithful.

Men will be able to accept the God made-man, only when they treat each other with mutual respect and care, as children of the same Father, called to live in *common unity*.

Chapter XI

AN IDENTITY OF THE HIGHEST DIGNITY

In general terms, our personal identity is what makes us who we are. And what we are is expressed through the works we do. Furthermore, our works not only reveal our identity, but also the identity of the person who taught them to us. Therefore, when we do the works of God, his identity becomes ours. This sharing of identities elevates man to one of the highest dignities in the universe.

1. Man's identity is united to God's identity

This is how this unity becomes a reality:

– By loving our enemies.
– By praying for those who persecute us (*Matthew* 5:44).
– By giving to those who ask.
– By giving, even beyond the limits of the requests. *"If anyone wants to go to law with you over your tunic, hand him your cloak as well. Should anyone press you into service for one mile, go with him for two miles"* (*Matthew* 5:40-41).

The fact that a person's works reveal the identity of another, demonstrates that the two are one. We identify ourselves with God by treating every person as equal, *"the bad and the good . . . the just and the unjust"* (*Matthew* 5:45). For all of us are children of the same Father, all of us are given the grace of sharing in the identity of God. Our failure to live in such a manner produces an absence of God in us. In other words, no one can turn the other cheek or love his enemies unless God lives in him.

It is because of the harm man causes others or because of his indifference toward another's suffering that he relinquishes his identity with God. However, God invites man to retake his identity.

Once we appropriate for ourselves the identity of God, we assume the responsibility (and privilege) of revealing our identity to all our fellow humans, who, in turn, will be able to see God in us. If we are to appropriate for ourselves the identity of God, we must always remain in him because without him, our human efforts, no matter how courageous they may be, will not afford us enough strength to love our enemies, and to pray for those who persecute us.

Once we all identify ourselves with God, we will attain the fullness of our identity, we will become *"perfect, just as [our] heavenly Father is perfect"* (*Matthew* 5:48), and we will become a true community just like God is trinitarian.

"The salt of the earth" and "the light of the world"

Jesus Christ describes the identity of a human being as *"the salt of the earth" and the "light of the world"* (*Matthew* 5:13-14), in recognition of our communitarian and unifying nature. Now, do we live up to it?

What does it mean to be the salt of the earth?

It means that every person has the ability to bring about goodness to humanity, to develop the universal human community's unity and freedom. This is how the earth is "seasoned" by the "salt of the earth": by *"setting free the oppressed, breaking every yoke; sharing your bread with the hungry, sheltering the oppressed and the homeless; clothing the naked when you see them, and not turning your back on your own, [on your fellow human beings]" (Isaiah 58:6-7).*

What does it mean to be the light of the world?

It means that every person who lives in accordance with the goodness of his human nature has the capacity to be a luminous example of life to the world. Nothing can remain in darkness when people live the goodness of their nature; they are shining lights when they live in unity and freedom.

"A city set on a mountain cannot be hidden. Nor do they light a lamp and put it under a bushel basket; it is set on a lampstand, where it gives light to all in the house" (Matthew 5:14-15). Likewise, the goodness of men created in the image of God cannot be hidden.

Those who are the light of the world *"shine through the darkness, a light for the upright; they are gracious, merciful and just. All goes well for those... who conduct their affairs with justice" (Psalm 112:4-5).*

What happens when men fail to live as "the salt of the earth" and "the light of the world"?

They lose their quality of being human because they lose their freedom, unity, and equality. This failure causes them to destroy their very human identity. *"But if salt loses its taste, with what can it be seasoned? It is no longer good for anything but to be thrown out and trampled underfoot" (Matthew 5:13).* If man fails to live in accordance with his own human nature, what is his life good for? It is good for nothing; it becomes the cause of his downfall.

2. Goodness is an essential element of human identity

Because men are the image of God, they must live in accordance with the goodness of their hearts, in accordance with the goodness that is innate in them, a goodness that is not the result of any external command. For God himself is by his own volition, all goodness, and only goodness does come out of him.

Along with God's goodness, men are also given *"free choice"* (*Sirach* 15:14) so they may be loyal to God's will by choosing to keep his commandments without any coercion, by choosing to seek the wellbeing of all humankind, and by choosing to live in unity, just as God lives. God's law does not coerce the will of men. They remain free to act according to their own volition: *"Before man are life and death, whichever he chooses shall be given him"* (*Sirach* 15:17). *"No man does [God] command to sin, to none does he give strength for lies"* (*Sirach* 15:20).

However, men chose their own self-serving interests, creating conflicts among themselves and resorting to the law (the coercive, external mandate) in order to "legalize" their established "order."

The law, imposed in this manner, determines what is right and wrong, what is good and evil, what is legal and illegal, and what is allowed and prohibited. Therefore, the law removes man's goodness from the realm of his heart and places it under the jurisdiction of an external, coercive mandate – the law. (The essence of the law is coercion, that is, the power to be enforced by punishment or any sort of harm. Without coercion the law ceases to be a law.) Consequently, man is no longer inspired by the goodness of the God who lives in his heart, but rather placed under the authority of an external law.

Christ comes to fulfill the law living in man's heart, not the external law that is an instrument of coercion.

In order to do so, Christ Jesus restores "his law" (the law, which since the beginning, has been an integral part of man's nature) in the heart of men. This is the law Jesus does not abolish, but fulfills (*Matthew* 5:17).

The law restored by God is fulfilled only by the men who, voluntarily, implant it in their hearts. Therefore, the strength of God's law rests, not in its letter (or coercion), but in the Spirit of he who offers it to us.

Men must regain the lost goodness of their hearts

If men are to live the true law of the Creator, that is, if they are to live in accordance with the inner goodness of their nature, they cannot continue to rule themselves by external mandates lacking internal righteousness. If we failed to do so, we will not attain common unity among ourselves. *"Unless your righteousness surpasses that of [those who impose and abide by coercive laws], you will not enter into the kingdom of heaven"* (*Matthew* 5:20).

Instances in which the external laws demonstrate their inadequacies, and how the goodness God implants in our hearts is the true fulfillment of the law (*Matthew* 5:21-28):

- The law says: *"You shall not kill; and whoever kills will be liable to judgment."* But God says: *"Whoever is angry with his brother is liable to judgment."*
- The law says: *"You shall not commit adultery."* But God says: *"everyone who looks at a woman with lust has already committed adultery with her in his heart."*
- The law says: you can *"bring your gift to the altar."* But God says you cannot offer a gift at the altar unless you *"go first and be reconciled with your brother."*

Who lack goodness?

"The rulers of this age" (*1 Corinthians* 2:6) are so entrenched in their external laws they can neither understand the goodness God has implanted in man's heart, nor can they understand God's wisdom, *"which God predetermined before the ages for our glory"* (*1 Corinthians* 2:7).

The rulers of this age will continue to void the goodness of man's heart as long as they continue to rule through external laws. We have the responsibility to restore the goodness of our hearts, goodness, which is the foundation for us to live in unity following the example of the trinitarian God.

3. Man's communitarian identity confronts obstacles along his evolution

Human evolution will follow a healthy path only if men, individually and collectively, strive at reaching the common good. The pursuit of our individual wellbeing is a trait of human nature, and so it is the pursuit of the wellbeing of the entire human collectivity. Therefore, human evolution will be in jeopardy if the fratricidal conflicts among men are not "cured". Along these lines, God is interested in the welfare of us individually and collectively. *"He cured many who were sick with various diseases, and drove out many demons"* (Mark 1:34).

Just as an individual gets sick, so does society

There are illnesses that afflict an individual person, and illnesses that afflict entire collectivities, such as the illnesses afflicting the people *"throughout the whole of Galilee"* (Mark 1:39).

Just as an individual may suffer gravely (even to the point of death) from an untreated illness, so does human society. The illnesses of human society, such as division and inequality can destroy the very fiber of humanity (even to the point of annihilation). These societal illnesses subject humanity to *"months [years or centuries] of misery"* (Job 7:3), make our days *"come to an end without hope,"* and make us believe that we *"shall not see happiness again"* (Job 7:6-7).

Jesus Christ cures humanity's illnesses

Our suffering humanity needs *to gather at Christ's door, pursue him, and follow him wherever he goes* (Mark 1:33, 36, 37) because he is ready to cure society's maladies; he *"heals the brokenhearted, binds up [humanity's] wounds . . . sustains the poor but casts the wicked to the ground"* (Psalm 147:3, 6); he frees humanity from all its ailments, and sets us on the path of a healthy human evolution.

Physical and spiritual wellbeing are characteristics of the human community

It is not enough to live well physically; it is also necessary to live well spiritually. One of the greatest offenses a person can commit against his fellowmen consists in depriving them of their right to live life to the fullest. God has endowed men with the inalienable right to live life to the fullest.

In the gospel of Mark, Jesus demonstrated that fullness of life involves both its physical and its spiritual aspects when he healed a paralytic man of all his ailments, beginning with his spiritual ailments (sin) and concluding with his physical ailment (paralysis) (*Mark* 2:1-12).

Spiritual health must be restored first because without it, physical health serves no purpose. Let us explain: a selfish person is by definition someone who lacks the ability to use his physical (or mental) attributes for the wellbeing of others. Thus, the absence of spiritual health is worse than the lack of physical capabilities.

Furthermore, through the miracle of the healing of the paralytic, Jesus reveals himself as someone who suffers the misunderstanding and persecution from those who denied the right to fullness of life. When Jesus told the paralytic: *"Child, your sins are forgiven"*, the scribes thought to themselves: *"Why does this man speak that way? He is blaspheming"* (*Mark* 2: 5-7).

Those who held authority in the times of Jesus (like those in our times) were ill with their own sins, the sins of being responsible for promoting inequality and oppression; sins they were able to hide from the sight of the people and cover up under the appearance of a "legal order."

They tried to limit the authority of God. They tried to take away his power to grant men fullness of wellbeing, physically and spiritually. However, the sight of the paralytic carrying his mat and going home (*Mark* 2:11) left no doubt in anybody's mind that Jesus has power over body and soul, and men have the inalienable right to fullness of life, both spiritually and physically.

God heals us totally so we may be capable of restoring what makes us whole persons, living in a lasting and fruitful human community.

4. The power of men within the community

In a human community, every one of its members shares in the power of their Creator. Obviously, his power is so great that some may feel overwhelmed by it. In the gospel of Luke, Peter says to Jesus: *"Depart from me, Lord, for I am a sinful man"* (*Luke* 5:8), in other words, Peter was fearful of the prospect of having the power of God at his disposal.

For those who are invited to share in the power of God, the idea of abusing God's powers may be quite frightening. What would the power of God do to a man's life? Would it make life more difficult or easier? Would it bring him successes or failures? Would he use such power to serve or to exploit his fellowmen? Would it bring him salvation or condemnation?

Jesus, however, addresses those concerns: *"Do not be afraid from now on you will be catching men"* (*Luke* 5:10). Which means an individual will not use God's power for his own personal gain, or his selfish interests; he will not use God's power in a sinful, unjust manner. Instead, he will use it for the benefit of all, as a true fisher of men.

In the world today, there are leaders (political, economic, military, etc.) who use the powers given them by God to pursue their own selfish interests, to attend to their thirst for wealth and domination, which in turn brings about injustice and oppression. Furthermore, those leaders not only choose to remain in their sinfulness by refusing to use their resources ("their boats and nets") for the benefit of all, but also by using them to enhance their abusive power. Consequently, the more abusive they become, the more do they divide and split the human race.

The division of men into rich and poor

The abuse of economic power brings about the division of men into rich and poor, division that tends to perpetuate itself inasmuch as those who have more are never satisfied with what they have.

God created men to be one in their human dignity and equal in their right to have their needs met. However, by dividing themselves into poor and rich, men go against the Creator's intent. *"Woe to you who are rich, for you have received your consolation"* (*Luke* 6:24).

Now, let us clarify some issues regarding the causes of the division of men into rich and poor:

A. **The possession of material goods, in itself, does not cause the division of men into poor and rich,** because it is God's design that every human being should possess what is necessary in order to meet his needs at the highest level required by his human dignity. It is only when men establish an unjust economic system that they cause their own division into rich and poor.

B. **Scarcity or abundance of material goods cannot cause the division of men into poor and rich:**

- Concerning scarcity (Insufficient quantities or lack of resources and goods), let us present the following example: a collectivity of, say, ten individuals, has 1,000 dollars – which is a very small amount to live on for a month. If two of those individuals take $990 for themselves, leaving the rest with only $10, then the division between rich and poor appears. Whereas, if each individual takes $100, then there are no rich and poor, though each share is small.

- Concerning abundance (Great quantities of resources and goods), let us assume that the same collectivity mentioned above has ten million dollars – which is a very large amount to live on for a month. The division of men in poor and rich will appear if just one of its members is deprived of what is necessary for him to meet his needs to the fullest.

C. **The production of material goods cannot cause the division of men into rich and poor.** When the goods produced by able people are shared with those who are unable to produce them (the sick, the weak, the orphan, the unemployed, etc.), there is no division into rich and poor. But if some of the able individuals appropriate for themselves the fruits of production, then the division of men into poor and rich appears.

Aspects of economic justice

Economic justice involves the following aspects:

- Payment of fair wages and salaries.
- Economic capacity to acquire the necessary economic goods.
- Respect of labor rights.
- Safe working environment.

- Freedom in the organization of labor unions.
- Justice in the participation in the ownership of the means of production.
- Respect of the human dignity of everyone involved in the process of economic production.

Why does economic justice promote unity?

Because economic justice ensures the harmonious participation of very person in the production, distribution, and consumption of the goods necessary for a dignified life. Economic justice eliminates the causes of division and antagonisms between men. For example, economic justice prevents the employers from appropriating for themselves what belongs to their workers, thus bringing to and end the inequalities between those who possess scandalous wealth and those who live in poverty.

We must achieve economic justice for if we do not, we will be fostering and perpetuating division in a vicious cycle of never-ending dimensions.

Chapter XII

THE SATISFACTION OF HUMAN NEEDS ACCORDING TO THE WIIL OF GOD

In their efforts to satisfy their physical needs, men have instituted socioeconomic systems, which, as history demonstrates, have, for the most part, failed to achieve their goals mainly because of their deficiencies in justice and equality. In spite of the fact that scientific and technological advances have greatly improved man's ability to produce abundant wealth and distribute it fairly, the interference from powerful economic groups have prevented the vast majorities of people from sharing in the economic bonanza.

Thus, in order to achieve economic justice, men must follow the example of God's justice, whose goal is the satisfaction of all human needs, both physically and spiritually. *"If God so clothes the grass of the field, which grows today and is thrown into the oven tomorrow, will he not much more provide for you, O you of little faith?"* (*Matthew* 6:30).

We must *"seek first the kingdom [of God] and his righteousness, and all these things [clothing, food, shelter and every necessity of life] will be given [us] beside"* (*Matthew* 6:33). Whenever people abide by the righteousness of God, they are bound to succeed in their goals of meeting all their needs. God provides for our needs as long as we share in his justice. *"Your heavenly Father knows that you need them all"* (*Matthew* 6:32).

1. Easier said than done

It is easy to say we listen to the voice of God, but to do the will of the Father is very difficult. *"Not everyone who says . . . 'Lord, Lord,' will enter into the kingdom of heaven, but only the one who does the will of [our] Father in heaven"* (*Matthew* 7:21). To those who say "Lord, Lord" but fail to do the will of the Father, Jesus tells them in reply: *"I never knew you. Depart from me, you evildoers"* (*Matthew* 7:23). Why is this answer so severe? Because unity among men is an element of God's will, and anyone who does not live accordingly is against God.

The following are some of those who say, "Lord, Lord," but fail to do the will of the Father:

- Those who say they love peace, but promote wars.
- Those who say they respect freedom, but oppress others.
- Those who say wealth should be for all, but keep it for themselves.
- Those who say technology should be used for peaceful purposes, but use it for war and destruction.
- Those who say they hold public office to serve others, but only serve themselves.
- Those who call themselves righteous, but lie for personal gain.
- Those who say they work for freedom, but defend tyrannical governments.
- Those who say all men are created equal, but take pride in their alleged "superiority" over others.

All they do is to cry out "Lord, Lord" while completely ignoring *the will of our Father in heaven*. Their hearts are far from God, and in his eyes, they are *"evildoers"* (*Matthew* 7:23), who build their nations on sand, nations, which will collapse and be completely ruined (*Matthew* 7:26, 27).

Those who do the will of the Father are:

- Those who foster unity and justice among men.
- Those who promote social order, labor justice, and equity in the distribution of wealth.

   – Those who keep the will of God in their hearts and souls
(*Deuteronomy* 11:18).

Words will be useless unless they are accompanied by deeds. We must go beyond the popular expression "easier said than done".

How can we begin to do the will of God?

By acknowledging that the world needs peace, by recognizing the urgency to end antagonisms, and by committing ourselves to restore the communitarian way of life. It is God himself who reassures us of the viability of such a commitment: *"Call on me in time of distress; I will rescue you"* (*Psalm* 50:15).

The obvious obstacle to our efforts to do the will of God is our own reluctance to admit that there will not be justice as long as there are people living in oppression and poverty. The main reason why we tend to deny the existence of injustice is our own misconception that everything is fine, therefore, there is no need to do the will of God. In many instances God's will is seen as a hindrance to the established "order" in the world.

This approach to God's will represents a denial of God himself. It is a belief that the God of unity and life has no purpose in our life or in the world. Those in most need of doing God's will, and bringing healing in their lives are, precisely, the ones who reject such healing: They are convinced they *"do not need a physician"* (*Matthew* 9:12).

The individual and social wellbeing that comes along by doing God's will is real because: *what he has promised he is also able to do* (*Romans* 4:21).

2. Doing the will of the Father involves a sacrifice and ends up in joy

To do the will of God involves a sacrifice on our part... and when his will is realized, we are filled with joy. When people live in peace and unity, there is no more need for sacrifices. For, what would be the purpose of sacrifice if the goal of any sacrifice has already been achieved? How could sadness exist if the causes for sadness have been eliminated?

"Can the wedding guests fast while the bridegroom is with them?" (*Mark* 2:19). *"But the days will come when the bridegroom is taken away from them, and then they will fast on that day"* (*Mark* 2:20).

The concept of sacrifice (referred to in the gospel of Mark as *fasting*) has a two-fold meaning:

- Suffering as the result of the absence of God.
- Suffering as a result of our struggles to bring God back to us.

In a world of widespread socioeconomic antagonism, the sources of joy are no longer present; injustices and inequalities have set in. While this state of evil persists, a radical transformation is required, because *"no one sews a piece of unshrunken cloth on an old cloak. If he does, its fullness pulls away, the new from the old, and the tear gets worse. Likewise, no one pours new wine into old wineskins. Otherwise, the wine will burst the skins, and both the wine and the skins are ruined"* (*Mark* 2:21-22).

Implementing partial changes in a radically unjust society is like trying to sew a piece of unshrunken cloth on an old cloak. The world must be transformed completely; otherwise, it will not be able to receive the *new wine* of unity and peace, for *no one pours new wine into old wineskins*.

During the time of struggle for transformation, *humanity will fast on that day,* until the restoration of the human community is completed. It is our responsibility to bring back *the bridegroom to the wedding,* to put an end to the state of division and mutual destruction, an end to all wars, and an end to the exploitation of man by man.

Once we "spouse" human unity and equality, we will have succeeded in bringing the bridegroom back to the wedding, where there is no need to fast, where there is no more need for sacrifices, where joy will be the jewel of humankind.

3. Human laws ought to be the reflection of God's will

By virtue of having been created in freedom, man's creations cannot infringe on the freedom he received from God. Consequently, God's laws and man's laws have the same foundation, inasmuch as they are the expression of the will of the Creator and the acceptance of the one who was created. In the relationship between man and God, both protect what they create: their preeminence over their own creations.

The gospel of Mark shows that the law related to the observance of the Sabbath exists for the benefit of man, insofar as it is an expression of the will of a God who respects the freedom of man. And neither God nor man would infringe upon human freedom and integrity. To imply that man is for the law he created is the equivalent of stating that man is ruled by his own creation. Just as man is not above God, so the law is not above man. Therefore, *the Sabbath was made for man, not man for the Sabbath"* (*Mark* 2:27). This hierarchy also manifests itself in the superiority of a society ruled by unity and equality over a society where class struggle is the norm.

The human community implies the eradication of socioeconomic antagonisms

The division of men into antagonistic groups is a betrayal to human nature. It confronts man against man; and when members of the human race are thus confronted, they become a threat to their own existence.

The threat of mutual destruction means a contradiction of God's creation. God created the human race to be one and undivided, whereas the existence of antagonistic groups means the opposite. In order to survive, men must necessarily seek unity, not division.

Respectful of human freedom, Christ alerts us to the dangers of division: *"If a kingdom is divided against itself, that kingdom cannot stand. And if a house is divided against itself, that house will not be able to stand"* (*Mark* 3:24, 25).

When humanity is divided in antagonistic groups, men are torn by strife and become promoters of self-destruction, their existence in jeopardy. Therefore, men must restore unity, for unity is their normal state of life. Humanity has the responsibility to preserve itself by returning to its primordial common unity, the unity intended by the Creator.

By their fruits you shall know them

When men are divided in antagonistic groups, they produce the fruits of mutual destruction. Whereas, when they live in unity, they produce the fruits of peaceful coexistence. *"A good tree does not produce rotten fruit, nor does a rotten tree produce good fruit. For every tree is known by its own fruit"* (*Luke* 6:43-44).

Furthermore, division prevents us from seeing what is beneficial to humanity. When a person is compelled to live in a society divided in antagonistic classes, he is rendered incapable of seeing what unity is, on account of the *"splinter in [his] eye"* (*Luke* 6:42). Whereas, he who leads others to live in a divided society, is unable to see what unity is, on account of the *"wooden beam in [his] own eye"* (*Luke* 6:42). *"The wooden beam"* is the inability to see and understand the essential unity and equality among human beings.

He who promotes division acts like *"a blind person [guiding] a blind person"* (*Luke* 6:39), for he displays a total lack of understanding of human nature and a total disregard for human unity. This blindness imposed on other human beings is supported by means of false teachings, to the point where the blindness seems to be irreversible. Consequently, men must reestablish unity among themselves. Unity they can find in the goodness of their own hearts, the goodness given to them by God since their creation, the goodness that allows them to produce good fruits.

4. Relationship between the will of the communitarian God and the will of the communitarian man

A relationship with God requires the recognition that there is something in common between God and us. God first took the initiative by becoming one of us, by demonstrating that we have much in common. In turn, when men live in common unity, they give testimony of God's communitarian life.

Those who, in society, hold positions of authority – like a centurion who has several soldiers under his authority (*Luke* 7:2) – ought to realize that there are commonalities between them and God: they both expect their will to be obeyed.

On earth, man has authority over Nature and society. This authority is based on the power given to him by God; this authority must respect the dignity of every person, and produce the common good. Similarly, the authority of God is based on the respect for everything he creates.

However, the powerful who misuse their authority, separate themselves from God and become unable to establish a meaningful relationship with him, precisely because they refuse to have any commonality with him. Indeed, they seem to be making every effort to contradict God's authority because instead of unity, they promote division; instead of service, domination; instead of peace, war.

As it is, a class society is a hostile environment for Christ Jesus to dwell in. The tragedy consists in that man misses the opportunity to share in the power of The Almighty. By acknowledging the many things that we have in common with God, we open the door to share in his power and use it for the benefit of all, just like the Creator uses it.

5. The will of God infuses in men a vocation to communitarian life

Inasmuch as man's vocation is a call to live in community, every human institution ought to allow him the opportunity to fulfill such vocation. Whenever our societal institutions fail to be instruments of unification, we have the responsibility of restructuring them in order to turn them into sources and manifestations of unity. In some instances, the institutions of the world are even detrimental to unity, for they contribute to and promote conflicts between men.

In order to turn our societal institutions into sources and manifestations of unity, we must:

- Understand what human life is.
- Be compassionate with one another so as not to destroy ourselves.
- Instill in every member of society a vocation to communitarian life.

In addition, it is necessary to understand that:

- Jesus has the power to restore life and integrity to an individual and to any social institution. Lucas, in his gospel, relates the case of a man whose life and the integrity of his family are restored: *"A man who had died was being carried out, the only son of his mother, and she was a widow... When the Lord saw her, he was moved with pity for her and said to her, 'Do not weep.' He stepped forward and touched the coffin... and he said, 'Young man, I tell you, arise!' The dead man sat up and began to speak, and Jesus gave him to his mother"* (*Luke* 7:12-15).

- Men should not break up the unity created and restored by God.
- When class antagonisms break up men's common unity, there are no obstacles God cannot overcome in order to keep alive man's vocation to unity, now and throughout history.

Chapter XIII

COMMUNITARIAN PRODUCTIVITY IS MEASURED BY THE PRESENCE OF UNITY BETWEEN MEN

The harder men work to maintain unity, the more productive they become for the benefit of the human community. In this respect, there is much work to do *but the laborers are few* (*Matthew* 9:37). Indeed, very few; because many people choose to close their eyes to the conflicts and divisions in the world. Many refuse to see that there is a great need for laborers to work on the harvest of unity.

Those who refuse to be laborers fall into three categories:

- Those who live so comfortably that their only interest is in maintaining the status quo.
- Those who are indifferent to the afflictions of others.
- Those who are under so much oppression that they have lost the means and energies to seek their liberation.

However, every person has the potential to become a laborer: *"Ask the master of the harvest to send out laborers to his harvest"* (*Matthew* 9:38). And the existing laborers may be willing to increase their productivity.

God equips his laborers properly

Those who commit themselves to working with God in the harvest of unity, receive from him *"authority over unclean spirits to drive them out and to cure every disease and every illness"* (*Matthew* 10:1). That is, they receive authority to confront those who promote conflict and division, and to bring an end to the evils of exploitation and oppression, which so pervasively afflict our world.

Along with their willingness, the laborers show strength in the struggle to realize harmony, equality and unity among men. This strength comes from faith in God, and this faith consists of:

A. Faith in the truth God has revealed to us, for he is the Truth. What he reveals by his words and his deeds, we must *"proclaim on the housetops,"* and what he says to us, we must *"speak in the light"* (*Matthew* 10:27). There is nothing hidden in what God reveals to us, there is no double talk, there is no lie. And, this is his truth: what he reveals to us is for the wellbeing of all.

B. Faith in the dignity of our human nature because there is nothing of greater value than a human being. *"Are not two sparrows sold for a small coin? Yet not one of them falls to the ground without your Father's knowledge. Even all the hairs of your head are counted. So do not be afraid; you are worth more than many sparrows"* (*Matthew* 10:29-30). There is nothing in the universe that deserves to be called children of God, except men.

C. Faith that nothing can harm us. The world can only harm the body *"but cannot kill the soul"* (*Matthew* 10:28). Those who suffer injustice may experience death in the body, whereas, those who promote injustice experience dead in their soul.

D. Faith that we are free from fear, even in the face of trials and tribulations, because God is with us: *"Do not be afraid of [men]"* (*Matthew* 10:26). *"Everyone who acknowledges me before others, I will acknowledge before my heavenly Father"* (*Matthew* 10:32).

Those who speak up on behalf of the trinitarian God, share in his *"gracious gift [overflowing] for the many"* (*Romans* 5:15). Whereas, those who fail to speak up on behalf of God, cause sin (injustice, exploitation, division) to enter the world, *"and through sin, death"* (*Romans* 5:12).

1. Men achieve unity through a process of inclusion an exclusion

Throughout their evolution, men did not need to theorize that they were united to each other, because, by virtue of sharing the same human nature, they were fully cognizant of their unity, which presented itself as a process of inclusion and exclusion.

- **By inclusion,** men were cognizant of their unity as integral members of humankind living in harmony and moving forward in their evolution. That is to say, men were capable of understanding that, without each other, it would have been impossible for them to develop as a human species. They all were included in the human collectivity.
- **By exclusion,** men were fully aware that nothing else in creation was equal to them. They knew of their superiority over all other living beings in Nature, and saw themselves as a unique collectivity of beings, whose unity excludes everything else that is not human. This allowed men to develop a sense of equality, which was real only in the community of human beings.

This unity between men lasted until the appearance of divisions and antagonisms within the human collectivity, which alienated their intrinsic unity.

The unity between men was, since its very inception, an image and likeness of the unity between God and man. And when men alienated their human unity, God became man so that men could restore their lost unity.

This is how the unity between man and God is manifested: *"Whatever you did for one of these least brothers of mine, you did it for me"* (*Matthew* 25: 40), *"Whoever receives you receives me, and whoever receives me receives* *the one who sent me"* (*Matthew* 10: 40). This is the unity men must demonstrate in their relationships with one another, which may also be expressed as follows: whoever receives any man, receives all men, and whoever receives all men, receives God.

Once we restore unity among all human beings, we will have restored our unity with God.

Tools needed to increase the productivity of the harvest of unity

Men have the means to plant the seeds of unity by utilizing simplest tools, such as, respect and mutual understanding. Elements, which are in contrast to the tools the world utilizes: dominion and conflict. Respect and understanding create unity, whereas conflict and dominion create division. Unity brings about prosperity and progress, whereas division brings about regression and annihilation. In the gospel of Mark, Jesus compares the Kingdom of God to something as simple as *"a mustard seed that, when it is sawn in the ground, is the smallest of all the seeds on the earth. But once it is sawn, it springs up and becomes the largest of plants"* (*Mark* 4:31, 32).

A united humanity begins with mutual respect and understanding between two human beings, and progresses until it comes to include all human beings without excluding anyone. The existence of antagonisms and divisions among people, on the other hand, is a barrier for the materialization of unity.

True progress towards a prosperous community is based, obviously, on men's ability to achieve unity. Whereas, in a divided society, even though the presence of riches may give the impression of prosperity, the only ones who are prosperous are the powerful, in detriment of the weak. Again, there is no community without the harmonious participation of all.

In order for humanity to attain true prosperity (material and spiritual), every human being must contribute to it in a way that each one may have the opportunity to plant the seeds of unity and harvest the abundance of a communitarian life.

2. Unity turns a community into a boat which never sinks

That boat will never sink because Christ Jesus is one of its passengers. In the world today, however, the boat of humanity is dangerously navigating through storms of fratricidal conflicts and inequalities. Just as Jesus has the power to calm the *violent storms* in the seas, so must we have the power to stop destroying one another. If we want to keep our boat afloat, we must keep in mind the following:

A. That Christ is with us *in our boat, the boat of humanity,* and he will not let us perish in *"a violent squall"* (*Mark* 4:37), in the violent conflicts prevalent between antagonistic socioeconomic classes.

B. That we have the ability to do the works of Christ (works of liberation) because we *"no longer live for [ourselves] but for him who for [our] sake died and was raised"* (*2 Corinthians* 5:15). It is up to us to use our power to ensure that our boat will not sink.

C. That God, the creator of heaven and earth, has everything under his authority. He says: *"I set the limits for [the sea] and fastened the bar of its door... Thus far shall you come but no farther, and here shall your proud waves be stilled!"* (*Job* 38:10-11). Our faith in the God of communitarian life will assure us that our efforts to remain unified will not fail and our boat will not sink.

3. The right to gainful work and the right to live in unity

The life of God in us makes us all equal, inasmuch as it confers upon us the same dignity (the dignity of God), notwithstanding our individual characteristics, which make us distinct from one another. Out of the uniqueness of each person, human equality is born, making humanity rich by the work and contributions of each individual. The uniqueness of each member is, therefore, a necessary condition to achieve human equality.

Humanity's richness is measured by the life of the trinitarian God in us; in other words, the God of all richness makes us always rich. *"For your sake [God] became poor although he was rich, so that by his poverty you might become rich"* (*2 Corinthians* 8:9).

Economic equality

One of the aspects of human equality is economic equality, which finds its ultimate foundation – as does any other aspect of equality – in the will of the Creator. This is how we achieve economic equality between men: *"as a matter of equality your surplus at the present time should supply [the] needs [of those who now are burdened], so that their surplus may also supply your needs [when you are burdened], that there may be equality. As it is written: 'Whoever had much did not have more, and whoever had little did not have less'"* (*2 Corinthians* 8:13-15).

Whenever God lives in us, he makes us all equal both in heaven and on earth:

A. Equality on earth manifests itself through common unity.
B. Equality in heaven manifests itself through the *"Communion of Saints,"* for the saints come to our aid here on earth to supply our needs for spiritual life whenever it is lacking in us.

Why does the work of the human community consist in maintaining equality? Because without equality we would cease to be who we are, and our destiny would be mutual annihilation. We must devote ourselves to living in common unity and equality, eradicating the divisions between powerful and weak, oppressors and oppressed, opulence and misery. Equality breeds unity, unity brings about community, and community brings us closer to our trinitarian God.

The more we embrace unity, the freer we become

Freedom is possible only when men acknowledge the fundamental unity of their human nature. The presence of inequalities (such as superior and inferior, privileged and deprived, exploiter and exploited, etc.) harms the freedom of all.

The gospel of Luke speaks of a sinful woman who *"began to bathe*

[the Lord's] feet with her tears. Then she wiped them with her hair, kissed them, and anointed them with the [perfumed] ointment" (*Luke* 7:37, 38).

This woman was fully cognizant that she had received a new life in freedom. She knew she had been freed from the burdens of her past, burdens that had impeded her to be part of her community. Now, as a free person, she felt moved to express her gratitude to the one who had liberated her, the one who had brought her back to the community. This expression of gratitude had to be as radical as the freedom she had regained. Similarly, those who return to communitarian life retake the freedom they had previously lost to enmities.

Who are not capable of living in freedom?

Those who fail to eliminate the barriers to unity, those who do not want to have a new life, those who deprive others of their freedom, those do not understand that no one can be free unless everybody is free.

What prevents them from seeing the barriers to freedom? The blindness caused by their own earthly power, which they revere and are grateful for. Therefore, it becomes quite impossible for them to accept a God who stands for freedom for all.

Those who reject the freedom that comes from God do not tolerate expressions of gratitude to God because they cannot understand why anyone should be thankful to him. The powerful of the world are critical of those who regain their freedom, because a free person is, in fact, a person freed from the oppressors of the world.

4. Those who partake of the intimacy of Christ live in unity between themselves

We all are invited to partake in the intimacy of Christ. We all are invited to know him as thoroughly as he knows us and to become one with him as he is one with the Father. Furthermore, our intimacy with Christ includes our intimacy with all human beings. Behold an expression of intimacy with Christ: every time we pray, we are with God and he is with us. *"When Jesus was praying in solitude, . . . the disciples were with him"* (*Luke*: 9:18).

Being in the intimacy of Christ is two-fold:

A. Jesus wants us to know him fully, because there can be no intimacy unless two people fully know one another. Jesus asks us, *"Who do you say that I am?"* (*Luke* 9:20). If we recognize him as the Christ, he will define for us who he truly is: he is *"the Son of Man [who] must suffer greatly, be rejected by [the powerful of the world], and be killed and on the third day be raised"* (*Luke* 9:22). This is the most thorough revelation of the God who invites us to become intimate with him, who wants us to know him exactly as he truly is.

B. Jesus wants us to know one another fully, exactly like we are: *"Children of God"* (*Galatians* 3:26). Just as Jesus is intimate with us, so we must be intimate with one another by living in unity, understanding, peace and equality; showing mutual concern for one another. The intimacy between human beings is predicated on the fact that God made himself one of us so that we may share fully in his life and become one with him.

A world divided into antagonistic classes, however, teaches that men should not be intimate with God, or with one another. This world promotes the sort of division and inequality that makes *the Son of Man endure many sufferings, rejects him and puts him to death* (*Luke* 9:22).

5. The human community is the proper environment for men to live in freedom

"For freedom Christ set us free" (*Galatians* 5:1). It is God's will to endowed man with freedom, and it is man's responsibility to remain free. Free from what? Free from everything that is against human dignity – free from destruction, free from oppression, free from greed, and free from selfishness. Otherwise, *"If you go on biting and devouring one another, [you will be] consumed by one another"* (*Galatians* 5:15).

The opposite of freedom is destruction. Freedom is our call to *"serve one another through love"* (*Galatians* 5:13). Destruction occurs when our selfish pursuits lead us to the elimination of anybody who may get in the way. The "freedom" which is used for destruction is *"freedom as an opportunity for the flesh"* (*Galatians* 5:13), an opportunity for exploiting one another, an opportunity to break up human unity.

Our struggle to attain and to remain in freedom

Attaining and remaining in freedom always involves a struggle. This struggle goes through three phases:

A. The struggle within our own selves in order to rid ourselves of selfishness, indifference, apathy, and greed.

B. The struggle to place ourselves at the service of one another and to eliminate any inclination to dominate others.

C. The struggle to avoid regression, which means to *"stand firm and not submit again to the yoke of slavery"* (*Galatians* 5:1).

Chapter XIV

COMMUNITY VS CLASS SOCIETY

*T*he **human community** is a form of life where men establish and develop their ability to relate to one another by exercising humility (as opposed to dominion). In the gospel of Matthew, Jesus speaks of humility as the foundation of communitarian life: *"Learn from me, for I am meek and humble of heart"* (*Matthew* 11:29). And embracing humility is a way to free men from the burdens of divisions and antagonisms: *"Come to me all you who labor and are burdened"* (*Matthew* 11:28), come me and share in my life.

Communitarian men follow the wisdom of God, which is based on meekness and humility: *"See, your king shall come to you; a just savior is he, meek, and riding on an ass, on a colt, the foal of an ass. He shall banish . . . the warrior's bow . . . and he shall proclaim peace to the nations"* (*Zechariah* 9:9-10).

Class society, on the other hand, is a way of life whereby the powerful of the world impose their rule by instituting "the wisdom of the world" (*Matthew* 11:25). The world uses its "wisdom" to justify injustice, to *"live according to the flesh"* (*Romans* 8:13). (The term *"flesh"* depicts the iniquities and injustices of a world that is in opposition to the life-giving Spirit). It follows, then, that those who follow the wisdom of the world cannot see or possess the wisdom of the communitarian God.

The meek and the humble of heart will live

Contrary to the world's wisdom, those who are *meek and humble of heart* can bring an end to the cycle of divisive power proper of a society ruled by conflict and antagonism. By sharing in the wisdom of God, the meek and humble can move forward toward the fulfillment of their communitarian nature: *"Come to me, all you who labor and are burdened, and I will give you rest. Take my yoke upon you and learn from me, for I am meek and humble of heart; and you will find rest for yourselves. For my yoke is easy, and my burden light"* (*Matthew* 11:28-30).

Deafness in a class society

It is not uncommon for men living in a class society to be deaf to the voice of God, even though he speaks to all of them, all the time, wherever they may be. In his gospel, Matthew presents God as a sower who sows the seed everywhere, *"some seed fell on the path... Some fell on rocky ground... Some seed fell among thorns... But some seed fell on rich soil"* (*Matthew* 13:4-8). What God says, is said to all.

To hear the word of God means to understand it. However, some people *"shall indeed hear but not understand... shall indeed look but never see. Gross is the heart of these people, they will hardly hear with their ears, they have closed their eyes"* (*Matthew* 13:14-15).

Why do they refuse to see and hear?

They refuse to see and hear *"lest they see with their eyes and hear with their ears and understand with their hearts and be converted, and I heal them"* (*Matthew* 13:15). Many choose not to see or understand how much misery division causes to people, they refuse to see and hear that the true wealth of the human race is based on the Word that speaks of unity, peace, and justice; the Word that advocates for mutual respect and the common good. They are the ones with *"gross hearts"* who refuse to possess the *"knowledge of the mysteries of the kingdom of heaven"* (*Matthew* 13:11). *"To anyone who has, more will be given and he will grow rich; from anyone who has not, even what he has will be taken away"* (*Matthew* 13:12).

To anyone who has respect for life, more life will be given; from anyone who has not, even what he has will be taken away.

1. Communitarian life through the History of Salvation

Humanity begins its existence like a *"good seed"* filled with the goodness instilled in it by its Creator. In the gospel of Matthew, Jesus likens the kingdom of heaven to *"a man who sowed good seed in his field"* (*Matthew* 13:24). And, as the sower expects a good harvest, so does humanity.

Now, if humankind begins as a good seed and ends as a good harvest, what happened in between? Evil enters the heart of man, causing humanity to distort human nature just like the planting of the weeds gave the field of good wheat a configuration different than the one intended by the owner of the field.

Evil in human society appears when people exploit one another, breaking their essential unity, just like the *"weeds appeared"* in the field (*Matthew* 13:26) mixed with the good seed. *"While everyone was asleep [the] enemy came and sowed weeds all through the wheat and then went off"* (*Matthew* 13:25).

God manifests his justice in human history

In following the line of thought of the parable of the Weed and the Wheat, it can be said that God's justice is, essentially, an act of restoration of human unity and a promise of liberation offered to all, both the righteous and the evildoers, throughout human history.

This is how God manifests his justice:

A. By pouring his goodness, not only at the time when he sows "good seed in his field" and when he "gathers the wheat into [his] barn" (that is to say, at the beginning and at the end of time), but also when he becomes a man, in order to offer his life for the salvation of humanity.

B. By respecting everyone's freedom, the freedom of the righteous as well as the freedom of the evildoers. The owner of the field orders his laborers not to pull up the weeds for *"if you pull up the weeds you might uproot the wheat along with them. Let them grow together until harvest"* (*Matthew* 13:29-30). It is God's design to allow men to be the authors of their own destiny: for life or for death. (Even unjust societies take upon themselves the "freedom" to grow by promoting the selfish "prosperity" of the dominant group, in the same manner the "weed" grows strong and reaches full maturity).

C. By offering his own Spirit to everybody, always: *"The Spirit ... comes to the aid of our weakness ... And the one who searches hearts knows what is the intention of the Spirit, because it intercedes for the holy ones according to God's will"* (*Romans* 8:26-27). In a world immersed in a culture of death, it is an act of justice for us to count on the strength of God's Spirit as a means of salvation, individually and collectively, thus, preventing our weaknesses from turning us into "weed."

D. By offering his own personal example: *"Your might is the source of justice; your mastery over all things makes you lenient to all ... Though you are master of might, you judge with clemency ... And you taught your people, by these deeds, that those who are just must be kind"* (*Wisdom* 12:16, 18, 19). Therefore, the All-merciful wants us to be merciful as well.

E. By giving us faith in him, for it is by faith that we are able to say: *"You, Lord are a merciful and gracious God"* (*Psalm* 86:15).

Will the powerful allow the weak to receive justice?

Inasmuch as the rich accumulate their wealth by appropriating for themselves the wealth produced by the laborers, the latter will be denied justice. In a class society, those who lack riches, tend to be marginalized. When God became man in Jesus, he was rejected by the powerful, not so much because he was God, but because he was a man of limited economic means. *"Is he not the carpenter, the son of Mary?"* (*Mark* 6:3) – they contended. *"And they took offense at him"* even though they had seen his miraculous works.

God comes to the world in the form of a man (a poor man indeed), precisely, to reveal that the dignity of people does not come from wealth nor riches but from their capacity to live in unity and equality. Jesus came to the world not only to reveal his divine nature, but also to reveal his human nature, nature of which we all participate. However, the revelation of his human nature caused Jesus to be rejected by men.

Thus, it came to happen that by rejecting Jesus, men planted the seeds of Calvary. Similarly, when we reject our fellow human beings, we placed them on a cross.

The advocates for unity, equality, and righteousness must deal with rejection. *"Son of man, I am sending you [to a people] . . . hard of face and obstinate of heart"* (*Ezekiel* 2:3-4). The "obstinate of heart" of our times are those who are intent on treating people as if they were objects (not human). The "hard of face" are those who cannot understand the greatness of human nature and fail to recognize their own human dignity.

Men can choose between the power of the human community or the power of class society. Let us describe both:

A. The power in the human community

The power in the human community comes from God: *Jesus "summoned the Twelve and began to send them out two by two and gave them authority over unclean spirits,"* over evil in all its forms (*Mark* 6:7). If we choose the power of God, we must also choose the means he puts at our disposal: compassion, personal commitment, and sincerity in placing the welfare of others before our own. In other words, we must utilize the means rooted in the goodness of our human nature. If we choose the power of God we must *"take nothing for the journey but a walking stick – no food, no sack, no money"* (*Mark* 6:8). This is a way to symbolize total detachment from the power and means of the world.

B. The power of class society

The power of class society is based on the strength to subjugate and dominate others, is predicated on the advantage of the strong over the weak. This power is an infringement against the dignity of those who fall under subjugation.

If we choose the power of class society, we will be bound to use its prescribed means and methods: domination and forceful imposition of our will upon others. Thus, instead of curing the illnesses of the world, we will be making them worse.

What happens when we choose the power of the human community?

"Prosperity will fill our land. Love and trust will meet; justice and peace will kiss. Truth will spring from the earth; justice will look down from heaven. The Lord will surely grant abundance; our land will yield its increase. Prosperity will march before the Lord, and good fortune will follow behind" (*Psalm* 85:10-14).

What does it mean to live in unity? It means to break down *"the dividing wall of enmity"* so those who were once enemies are no longer enemies by virtue of the personal example and sacrifice of the one who promotes unity. When a person lives in unity with another person, he creates *"in himself a new person in place of the two"* (*Ephesians* 2: 14, 15).

Those who preach unity and promote division

"Woe to the shepherds who mislead and scatter the flock." To them God says, *"I will take care to punish your evil deeds"* (*Jeremiah* 23:1-2). Those who preach unity but fail to live in unity bring about confusion, darkness and all sorts of individual and collective maladies. They place barriers between men and God.

On the contrary, he who preaches unity and lives in unity *"shall reign and govern wisely, he shall do what is right and just in the land"* (*Jeremiah* 33:15), he will share in the life of a God whose name is: *"The Lord our justice"* (*Jeremiah* 23:6).

2. Communitarian unity is the fruit of individual diversity

On the one hand, all men are equal because they share one and the same human nature. On the other hand, no two men are identical because each one of them has distinct individual characteristics. It is by the exercise of their own individual characteristics that the multitude of individuals contribute to create the unity of the human community. Yes, many members, one body! This is what the apostle Paul explains in reference to Christ and the members of his universal Church: *"a body is one though it has many parts, and all the parts of the body, though many, are one body... The eye cannot say to the hand, 'I do not need you' nor the head to the feet, 'I do not need you'... God has constructed the body as to give greater honor to a part that is without it, so that there may be no division in the body, but that the parts may have the same concern for one another. If [one] part suffers, all the parts suffer with it; if one part is honored, all the parts share its joy. Now you are Christ's body, and individually arts of it"* (*1 Corinthians* 12: 12, 21, 24-27).

In the human community, its members do not lose their individual identity; on the contrary, they enrich it by virtue of their contribution to the communitarian cohesiveness. The higher the quality of the individual contribution, the greater will be the quality of the communitarian body. Now, a point must be made clearly, that human individualities do not create antagonistic classes because diversity leads to unity, except, of course, when men use their individualities to exploit their fellowmen.

3. Those who live in unity bear the marks of Christ

To bear the marks of Christ means to make God visible to the world (*Galatians* 6:17). That is to say, those who live in unity and peace make possible for the world to see that the trinitarian God lives in them. However, in a class society, the bearers of the marks of Christ are treated *"like lambs among wolves"* (*Luke* 10:3).

The wolves of the world would not believe in the marks of Christ, even if they were to see them; instead, they believe in their *"money bags"* (*Luke* 10:4), in the wealth they have appropriated for themselves, and in the worldly power coming from material possessions. In their eyes nothing can be achieved without money, and anyone who does not pursue money, is a failure. To them, money is the clearest mark of worldly success, even though money is the "mark" of men's division in rich and poor.

The marks of Christ are efficacious

Those who bear the marks of Christ bring unity to people, eradicate divisions, and announce: *"The kingdom of God is at hand for you"* (*Luke* 10:9).

In order to disarm *the wolves of the world*, Christ advises his disciples: *"carry no money bag"* (*Luke* 10:4). Because money is the means *par excellence* of an economic system based on accumulation of wealth for selfish purposes.

Love of neighbor is one of the "marks" of Christ

Who is our neighbor? Every person is our neighbor! No one is excluded.

However, a class society tends to exclude those who do not share the same ideas with the powerful class, those who have fallen in disgrace, those who suffer, those who try to stop the injustices perpetrated by the dominant class, and those who are the victims of oppression. For such a society, neighbor is not the *"man who fell victim to robbers"* (*Luke* 10:30).

Our neighbor is more clearly revealed in the person of the victim because the victim is in more dire need of compassion; the victim is the product of the wrongdoings or indifference of other human beings.

The man who fell victim to robbers is a neighbor to all, but only the "Good Samaritan" treated him as a neighbor. The Samaritan felt compassion for the victim and exposed two types of wrongdoings:

A. The wrongdoings of those who physically hurt the victim; and
B. The indifference of those who did nothing. Indifference has the same effect as the wrongdoings of those who caused the harm in the first place (the victim remained half-dead because of those who were indifferent). Those who are indifferent in front of a suffering person are responsible of a form of aggression inasmuch as they deprive their neighbor of what he needs.

To ignore the victim is to cover our eyes so as not to see the plight of the suffering and pretend that we live in a "wonderful world."

Why do the wrongdoers ignore the victim?

Because the suffering of the victim is the product of the actions or lack of action of the wrongdoers themselves. Paradoxically, as the victims become more visible, greater does the need become for the wrongdoers to ignore their victims.

To love our neighbor is a requisite to love God

Anyone who loves his neighbor is on the side of God, and anyone who is on the side of God has chosen the best part of life (*Luke* 10:42). Love of neighbor and love of God are inseparable insofar as both loves are integral parts of an unbreakable unity. Tragically, in the world of antagonistic socioeconomic classes, the relationships between men tend to lead them to harming one another, thus, making a mockery of love of neighbor and, consequently, impairing man's relationship with God.

Love of neighbor makes possible for us to know the communitarian God living in us in intimate unity. Without love of neighbor, life becomes an endless chase after selfish interests, and a sure means to ignite confrontations. That is, precisely, the picture of a society divided in antagonistic classes.

When men choose to love neighbor and God, they have chosen the best part of life, and that life *"will not be taken away from [them]"* (*Luke* 10:42).

Chapter XV

COMMUNITARIAN LIFE IS A TREASURE

1. Why is communitarian life a treasure?

*B*ecause living in peace and unity is truly a treasure. How do we begin to possess this treasure? By having *"a listening heart … to distinguish between good and evil"* (*1 Kings* 3:9).

This treasure consists in living in accordance with the law of God, which *"is more precious to me than heaps of silver and gold"* (*Psalm* 119:72). *"Truly I love your command more than the finest gold. Thus, I follow all your precepts"* (*Psalm* 119:127-128). This treasure *"sheds light, gives understanding to the simple"* (*Psalm* 119:130), to those whom the world considers undeserving of being counted as members of the human community.

Understanding the law of God is a treasure, which is worth more than *long life and riches* (*1 Kings* 3:11), is worth more than any kind of worldly power.

However, this treasure is not easy to find because it is hidden under:

- Half-truths the world promotes as being true. It is extremely difficult to find the treasure in a world where the truth is manipulated in order to create confusion and division among people.

- False sense of happiness. It is extremely difficult to find the treasure in a world that teaches that the only source of happiness comes from the possession of material wealth.
- Deceptive promises. It is extremely difficult to find the treasure in a class society that promises what it cannot deliver.

If we are to find the treasure, we must be motivated to do so

The following is required to find the treasure:

- We must be motivated to accept that every person is a member of the human community. *"I serve you [God] in the midst of the people whom you have chosen"* (*1 Kings* 3:8), that is, in the midst of humanity.
- We must be motivated to accept our role as servants to our fellowmen. In order to possess the treasure, one must be a *servant* to all (*1 Kings* 3:6).

Once we find the treasure, we must be willing to give up everything else in order to keep it. In the gospel of Matthew, Jesus uses the following analogy: When a person finds a treasure buried in a field, he *"goes and sells all that he has and buys that field"* (*Matthew* 13:44). That is, the finder must give up anything that is a negation of that treasure. The finder must give up worldly riches and abusive power.

What happens once we possess the treasure?

The person (or nation) who comes to possess the treasure becomes the recipient of the communitarian God's goodness: *"All things work for good for those who love God"* (*Romans* 8:28).

2. The treasure facilitates the cooperation between God and man

Whenever men live in unity and peace with one another, they are capable of recognizing their own needs as well as the compassion of

God. Matthew, in his gospel, presents the Feeding of the Multitude as an event consisting of three elements: man's need for food, Christ's compassion before this need, and the cooperation between God and men:

A. Five thousand people are in need of food and lack the resources to feed themselves.

B. Christ's *"heart was moved with pity for them"* (*Matthew* 14: 14)

C. Now, this is how the cooperation between Christ and men develops: Initially the disciples try to evade their responsibility to feed the hungry – they say: *"dismiss the crowds"* (*Matthew* 14:15). Christ, however, responds: *"There is no need for them to go away; give them some food yourselves"* (*Matthew* 14:14-16). In other words, given the circumstances, we have the means to satisfy others' needs if we cooperate with Jesus. No matter how little we may have – *"Five loaves and two fish are all we have here"* (*Matthew* 14:17) –, Christ always takes whatever we have, he always accepts our cooperation, and he always kindles the fire of compassion in our hearts.

Christ accepts what we give him

The miracle of the Feeding of the Multitude involves our readiness to follow God's will and to give him our resources, whatever little they may be. The only answer unacceptable to God is: *"dismiss the crowds"* or "there is nothing we can do."

Christ shows us what to do with the resources we have

Jesus always says: Whatever little you may have, *"bring them here to me"* (*Matthew* 14:18), then he shows us that the wealth of the world is to be used for the benefit of all. We know the five loaves and the two fish could have been enough to feed, say, seven or nine people, but if that had been the destiny of the loves and the fish, then the crowds would have gone away hungry.

Through the cooperation between God and man, everyone received food; all *had their fill* (*Matthew* 14: 20). Men may multiply wealth many times over, but if such wealth is not used for the benefit of all, humanity will remain hungry.

How do those, who hold worldly power, handle the world's resources?

They make the same request: "Bring them here to me," but – here is where the tragedy begins – they keep the *five loaves and two fish* for themselves, depriving the crowds of what they need.

The various types of socioeconomic systems instituted by men have, so far, failed to distribute the economic goods (*"the loaves and the fish"*) with justice among the people because egotistic minorities have appropriated for themselves the goods produced, while the vast majorities have gone hungry.

In order to produce and distribute the economic goods (*the loaves and the fish*) in accordance to the will of God:

A. We must understand the needs of our fellow human beings.
B. We must be *moved with pity* at the sight of starving multitudes (or at the sight of any human suffering).
C. We must respect equality within the universal human community because we all are children of the same Father who asks for our cooperation.

In order to cooperate with God, we must first find him

Where do we find God? In the gentle breeze, in the *"tiny whispering sound"* (*1 Kings* 19:12), in the voice *that proclaims peace to the people, in the place where love and truth meet, where justice and peace kiss* (*Psalm* 85: 9, 11).

However, when men divide themselves in conflicting socioeconomic classes, they are faced with great difficulties in finding God because they look for him where he is not, namely:

– God is not in the *"strong and heavy wind… rending the mountains and crushing rocks"* (*1 Kings* 19:11), but the dominant classes see their god in the power of wealth "rending and crushing" human equality.

- God is not in the powerful *"earthquake"* (*1 Kings* 19:11), but the ruling class sees its god in the devastating policies that reduce to rubble the rights to freedom, to employment, to housing, to health care, to education, to the protection of the family, among others.
- God is not in the scorching *"fire"* (*1 Kings* 19:12), but the powerful classes see their god in the scorching fire produced by weapons that make it possible for the strong to destroy the weak.

Because of its inability to see God, a class society resembles a boat in the process of sinking. A boat Christ approaches, walking on the sea (*Matthew* 14:22), in order to save it, in the hope that its passengers may see him as he truly is.

3. Quality of life is a communitarian treasure

In medical terms, *"quality of life"* usually refers to an improved level of physical and mental health, which allows a person to go on living with a comfortable or acceptable degree of self-sufficiency and a minimal level of pain, despite the existing pathologies. In socioeconomic terms, quality of life refers to a high standard of living as a result of men participation in the material wealth produced by the members of the human community.

The concept of quality of life, however, has a much broader significance as it encompasses all the aspects of human life, such as, physical, mental, spiritual, social, economic, political, and so on. Above all, quality of life refers to the quality of our relations with other persons and with God.

We reach the highest quality of life when we *"live in a manner worthy of the call [we] have received, with all humility and gentleness, with patience, bearing with one another through love, striving to preserve the unity of the spirit through the bond of peace: one body and one spirit"* (*Ephesians* 4:1-4). This quality of life is humankind's true treasure.

A life of the highest quality involves the following:

- A life of humility, that is, a life whereby all men are equal. True humility is the recognition of our equality, in that we all share the same human nature, nothing more and nothing less.

- A life of gentleness, that is, a life of mutual respect. Gentleness is the courage to respect one another.
- A life of patience, that is, a life whereby we never give up, even though our efforts to bring about equality may not be immediately fruitful.
- A life whereby we support one another, accept one another in our efforts to strengthen the unity among us. That is true love.
- A life of peace, that is, a life whereby no one causes any harm to anyone, whereby everything is done in the best interest of one another.

In order to achieve quality of life is necessary to be *"hungry"* for life

To be hungry for life means to want life-giving food, to care for life, to respect life, to share it with one another in equality and unity, because this is how life grows. Jesus Christ gives us the food that does not perish, *"the food that endures for eternal life"* (*John* 6:27); and, that food is himself, for he is *"the bread of life"* (*John* 6:35).

When we eat the bread of life, we transform our "old self" into our "new self" (*Ephesians* 4:24). The old self hungers for *futility of mind, darkened understanding, alienation from the life of God, ignorance, hardness of heart, callousness and licentiousness for the practice of every kind of impurity and excess* (*Ephesians* 4:17-19). The old self intentionally feeds himself with the lies that keep him from seeing the truth.

The new self, on the other hand, hungers for *"righteousness and holiness of truth"* (*Ephesians* 4:24). To the new person, truth is the conformity of his life with the life of God.

The man, who clings onto his old self, is not hungry for true life because he is mostly concerned with self-serving interests, with accumulating wealth for himself, with growing in power and dominion over his fellowmen. True hunger for life involves the understanding that a person's life is intimately and inseparably connected with the life of everyone else.

Humanity must be hungry for the kind of life that turns the old self into the new self. If we fail to awaken that hunger, then our world will die of starvation.

The closer we are to God, the greater the quality of our life

In a divided society, whenever God gets too close to man, the latter becomes uncomfortable – very uncomfortable. Why? because those who disdain human unity tend to reject the God of unity. God, in turn, not only becomes man in Christ but also becomes food for men to eat: *"I am the living bread that came down from heaven"* (*John* 6:51). In order to eat the *living bread*, man must give up the "food" the world feeds on, namely, the food of selfishness.

The foods of the world fail to restore man's dignity, fail to make him wholesome. *"This is enough, O Lord! Take my life for I am no better than my fathers"* (*1 Kings* 19:4). Then the Lord gives man the living bread through which he can be better than his fathers, through which he can have a better life, a life of the highest quality.

Without the living bread *"the journey will be too long for"* us (*1 kings* 19:7). If we continue to eat the man-made foods, we will be *"no better than [those who preceded us]"* (*1 Kings* 19:4).

What does it mean to eat the living bread?

Eating *the living bread* means to be *"kind to one another, compassionate, forgiving one another as God has forgiven [us] in Christ"*; it means getting rid of *"all bitterness, fury, shouting, and reviling… along with all malice"* (*Ephesians* 4:31-32).

The reason for us to eat the living bread is so we may be close to God, in a relationship whereby our human life is united to the divine life.

Man's aspiration to be united to God's life

Our desire to share in God's life begins its realization by asking him to come to us. To ask him *"Your kingdom come"* (*Luke* 11:2) implies that we know what is going on in God's kingdom. If someone does not know what is happening in the kingdom, how could he ask God for the coming of his kingdom?

To ask God, "Your kingdom come" also implies asking him "Your will be done on earth as it is in heaven." Now, we must ask ourselves, what is happening in his kingdom that we want to replicate here on earth? Do we truly want the events of the world to conform to the events of heaven? Are we sincere when we ask that life on earth be like life in heaven?

What is done in heaven is the will of God. And, what is the will of God? His will is: peace, compassion, unity, mutual respect, justice, equality, freedom, and so forth.

Is that what we truly want on earth?

We can say, unequivocally, that the unjust men of the world do not want this at all. It goes against their own interests and undermines their very existence on earth. It is impossible for those who exploit their fellow human beings to honestly say, "Your kingdom come; your will be done on earth as it is in heaven."

Only those who strive for peace, justice, equality, unity, compassion, mutual respect, and freedom can say "Your kingdom come; your will be done on earth as it is in heaven," because they know what is done in heaven and want the same to be done on earth.

4. The communitarian treasure enriches everybody, economically and emotionally

Depending on the way we use material possessions, they can contribute to unity or to division. If possessions are used for the benefit of all, they bring about unity. Whereas, possessions accumulated in the hands of a few and used for the benefit of a few, with the exclusion of others, bring about division. In other words, the communitarian use of wealth enriches humankind, whereas, its use for the exclusive benefit of the dominant class, brings about poverty to the vast majorities.

The greed of the *"rich man"* (*Luke* 12:16)

Greed moves the rich person to acquire his wealth through:

- Accumulation of material goods in excess of what he needs to meet his needs (*Luke* 12:17); and

- Dispossession of the workers who produced the material goods. The "bountiful harvest" (*Luke* 12:16) was certainly the product of the laborers, whose fruits ended up in the hands of the rich man (*James* 5:4)

The economic systems prevalent in the world have institutionalized the division of men in poor and rich, causing the fragmentation of the human race, and maintaining a world "order" contrary to the Creator's order. The greed for possessions has moved men away from God, has given possessions a greater value than that of men themselves, and has turned men into actual worshipers of their own possessions. We must end *"the greed that is idolatry"(Colossians* 3:5). That is, we must stop using possessions as a source of division between men and between men and God. We can achieve this by using our possessions for what they are intended, namely, for unity among all.

It is our responsibility to bring an end to our *old self* and restore our *new self* by building a world where possessions do not have a greater value than that of a human being.

From the point of view of man's emotional wellbeing, unity is a treasure which helps us to eradicate our fears.

"Do not be afraid any longer" (*Luke* 12:32).

What is the world afraid of?

When men are divided (into antagonistic socioeconomic classes, for instance), they are confronted with disturbing fears such as:

- The fear of insecurity. This fear is the result of the uncertainties and anxieties from impending threats, such as, "will I be the next one to be eliminated?" "Will I be the next victim of dispossession?" "Will I lack the means to meet my needs?"
- The fear of isolation. This fear results from the possibility that we may suffer abandonment by our friends or relatives; the possibility that we may suffer the emptiness of a selfish and

indifferent world; the possibility that we may find ourselves without personal identity.

- The fear of lack of fulfillment. This fear affects especially those who promote oppression against their fellowmen. It affects those who live in opulence and become increasingly fearful of life ending its biological course.

- The fear of confusion. This fear results from our inability to understand the truth. The truth being that human life is a life of unity and equality among all. However, in a world where men live divided by antagonisms, there is no way to justify that situation; but it can be "effectively" imposed upon people through confusion. And with confusion, fear sets in.

A fragmented society tries to address fear through a false sense of security

In order to relieve peoples' fears, the world offers a false sense of security through:

- The power of wealth, with the expectation that wealth may solve all our problems and give us security. However, when men are divided, the wealth accumulated in a few hands intensifies the insecurity of those who live in deprivation.

- The political power, with the expectation that the law may establish justice for all. However, there can be no justice whenever the law is utilized as an instrument to legalize a status quo based on injustice.

- The power of technology, with the expectation that, through technological means, we may be able to eradicate hunger, diseases, poverty, and other maladies. However, in a world of egotistic individuals and self-serving interest groups, technological advances, as a rule, fail to benefit the economically disenfranchised.

In Luke's gospel, Jesus says: *"Do not be afraid any longer, little flock, for your Father is pleased to give you the kingdom"* (*Luke* 12:32); a kingdom where human beings have nothing to fear; a kingdom where all live in unity and equality; a Kingdom where we all have one Father. There will be no fear whenever all men, without exception, are able to reclaim for themselves the benefits of their own creations, be it economic, political, technological or of any other nature.

Chapter XVI

THE HUMAN COMMUNITY ALLOWS MAN TO HAVE A VISION OF GOD

1. The human community is the environment for men to see and know God

If we accept that God created man in his image and likeness, we must also accept that to know man, necessarily, implies to know God. This type of relation presents an existential challenge to us because the more we know our creator, the more we will know ourselves, individually and collectively. And, the most appropriate environment for reaching this knowledge is the human community.

John, in his gospel, indicates that to see Jesus is as real as to see the Father. Jesus says: *"Whoever has seen me has seen the Father"* (*John* 14: 9). The entire Good News is the revelation that Jesus has come to the world so that men may know the Father: *"If you knew me, you would know my Father also"* (*John* 8: 19).

Throughout our life, Jesus Christ is constantly asking us the question: *"Who do you say that I am?"* (*Matthew* 16:15). In order to answer this question, men must refer to the time of their own creation, when God created them in his image and likeness, and when men could look at themselves and find the image and likeness of God in them. However, men departed from that image and likeness, and now, it is difficult for them to know God.

Whoever aspires to live in *common unity* will continue to respond, "God is my Father" made flesh in Jesus, who comes to restore, in us, the unitarian image and likeness of God. Once we acknowledge who God is, he will tell us that we are the ones he needs in order to bring all men back to him (*Matthew* 16:18), and that nothing will separate us from him. With the reassurance of knowing who we are, we assume the task of reminding others of who they are.

We come to know our true human identity when we share in the identity of God, and since he shares his identity with all of us, we are also to share our identity with all. For that reason, anyone who acknowledges that God is the creator and redeemer of all is also acknowledging that God lives in all of us.

By knowing God, we come to know that our life is the ongoing work of God in us, helping us to reinstate the initial order of unity and equality (in which God created us), and against which *the netherworld shall not prevail* (*Matthew* 16:18).

Man's responsibility to make God visible before the world

He who takes upon himself the task of making God visible before the world must be prepared *to take up his cross* (*Matthew* 16:24). That is, to take up the sufferings he will endure in his struggle against a world that has harmed such basic elements of human dignity as unity and equality. Therefore, there is a cross to be carried by those who pursue the restoration of unity and equality.

In his condition of being the Son of God, Jesus Christ *"suffered greatly from the elders, the chief priests, and the scribes [the powers of that time], and [was] killed"* (*Matthew* 16:21). Thus, it is inevitable that those who stand for what the Son of God stood for, will also suffer at the hands of those who, nowadays, hold the power of the world and the power to harm human dignity and foster division and inequality.

We cannot afford to be accomplices to the world: *"Do not conform yourself to this age"* – the age of evil (*Romans* 12:2). *"I urge you, therefore, brothers, by the mercies of God, to offer your bodies as a living sacrifice, holy and pleasing to God"* (*Romans* 12:1).

Those who take upon themselves the task of making God visible before the world must be cognizant of the fact that the ensuing struggle is inevitable and necessary:

- It is inevitable because those who hold the power of the world are not about to change their ways, and are willing and ready to utilize all the means at their disposal to preserve the status quo.
- It is necessary because it is the only way to restore unity and equality in the human community.

A difficult and inescapable responsibility. The prophet Jeremiah says: *"The word of the Lord has brought me derision and reproach all the day. I say to myself I will not mention him, I will speak in his name no more. But then it becomes like fire burning in my heart"* (*Jeremiah* 20:8, 9).

Our efforts to make God visible confront three obstacles:

A. Our growing frustrations resulting from the apparent inefficacy of our efforts.

B. The world's increasing indifference before human suffering.

C. The world's blatant violation of human unity and equality.

Matthew, in his gospel, describes the efforts of a suffering mother who begs Jesus to cure her sick daughter (*Matthew* 15: 21-28). While Jesus cures the daughter, the disciples showed disregard for the mother's pleas, and simply asked Jesus: *"Send her away, for she keeps calling out after us"* (*Matthew* 15:23).

The disciples' attitude resembles that of the powerful groups in class societies. The powerful suffer from callousness and indifference before human suffering.

Now, the mother – as seen in the gospel – demonstrates the kind of faith, effort, persistence, and endurance that are pleasing to God. *"O woman, great is your faith! Let it be done as you wish."* And so it happened, *"her daughter was healed from that hour"* (*Matthew* 15:28).

Can those who suffer from lack of compassion be healed from their callousness and indifference? Are they capable of been sensitive to the sufferings of others?

The overwhelming presence of societal maladies in the world cannot make us falter in our faith. On the contrary, those maladies are a good reason for us to grow in faith (a faith like that of the mother who asks for the healing of her daughter); a faith that will give us strength and endurance; a faith that will give us power to eradicate injustice and thus, allow us to make God visible before the world.

2. Can man focus his vision on God?

Men not only can set their vision on God, but they can also join him in a union of the most intimate nature. The New Testament uses the expression "to eat the flesh and drink the blood of Christ" in order to emphasize that the purpose of setting our eyes on God is to enter into a community with him. *"I say to you unless you eat the flesh of the Son of Man and drink his blood, you do not have life within you"* (*John* 6:53). We need to take God's life because we lack true life.

God tells us: *"To him who lacks understanding, I say, come, eat of my food, and drink of the wine I have mixed! Forsake foolishness that you may live, advance in the way of understanding"* (*Proverbs* 9:4-6). Fully cognizant that we lack true life and the ability to understand true life, we must hear the voice of the God made-man saying: I am *"the bread that came down from heaven . . . Whoever eats this bread will live forever"* (*John* 6:58). Christ wants us to fully understand that we can truly possess his life, just as by the action of "eating and drinking" a person can nurture his physical life.

Our world is lacking in life: *"These are evil days"* (*Ephesians* 5:16) because man's life has become radically distorted, and what is death, is taken as if it were life. Such is the case when war is chosen over peace, when the appropriation of wealth by a few is acceptable in spite of producing the impoverishment of many.

We must *"not continue in ignorance, but [must] try to understand what is the will of the Lord"* (*Ephesians* 5:17). The world seems to ignore the struggle between good and evil; the struggle between those who advocate for justice and peace and those who choose to live in destructive exploitation. It is up to us to grow in the understanding of life so we may be able to take the life of God if we want to live.

What is the benefit of seeing God?

The benefit is God himself, the second Person of the Trinity, the God who gives himself completely to us: *"My flesh is true food, and my blood is true drink"* (*John* 6:55). This means, whenever we accept God's offer, we take for ourselves his truth, totally, for he is total truth; we become free for he is true freedom; we become people of service and peace because he is true service and true peace; we become people of compassion and justice because he is true compassion and true justice. Without this truth, humanity cannot go on living.

It follows then, that *"unless you eat of the flesh of the Son of Man and drink his blood, you do not have life within you"* (*John* 6:53). When God offers himself to us, he seeks complete unity with us: one body, one blood. To accept God's offering implies a commitment from us to establish unity with our fellow human beings, which is the only requisite for us to accept unity with God.

In response to the proposition the Son of Man makes, men usually respond: *"This saying is hard; who can accept it?"* And those who reject it *"return to their former way of life"* (*John* 6:60, 66). That is, to their life of antagonism, divisions, emptiness, and self-destruction.

What is the response of those who have their eyes set on Christ?

They commit themselves to a life of unity by being *"subordinate to one another out of reverence for Christ"* (*Ephesians* 5:21). That is, by relating to one another as God relates to humankind. Our commitment to the trinitarian God is a commitment to live in *common unity* with men... and with God.

How do we establish unity with Jesus Christ?

A. By accepting him in our heart, that is, by believing that he is in us. Consequently, life becomes an exteriorization of what we have within us, and what comes out from us is God himself. When we allow God to live within us, we acquire the ability to bring the life of God into the world through the testimony of our own life.

B. By consciously and freely accepting that God's commandments are in our heart, in our inner self. That is to say, God's commandments are not external nor foreign to us because the enforcement of external commandments always implies an imposition, which denies the option to accept or reject. External laws carry a coercive punishment if they are not obeyed. And any imposition is incompatible with the unity God intends to establish with us. Such imposition hinders our spiritual and emotional maturity.

C. By our commitment to bring the life of the trinitarian God to humankind. When God lives in us, our works are the expressions of the unifying God who lives in us. And as we organize ourselves in society, our institutions must have the same spirit of the God who lives in us.

3. What can we do when we come to know Christ?

We can change the world! *"I have come to set the earth on fire, and how I wish it were already blazing!"* (*Luke* 12: 49). "To set the world on fire" is a symbolic way of saying that the earth is in need of radical change because the injustices and divisions among men are deeply rooted.

The need of change is, in itself, a cause of division among people:

- Those who believe the world is in no need of change say: "Everything is just fine for me, I have everything I need, and then some."
- Those who believe our world is in dire need of change say: "We must restore peace and unity in our world." Indeed, the need for change is so radical that such change is the equivalent of "setting the earth on fire." This is the reason God comes to the world.

Therefore, Christ himself is a cause of division. When God announces his plan to rescue the world from evil, people become divided: those who side with him and those who oppose him. This division is not just one of a separation between the two sides, but rather of a radical confrontation between them.

Both sides are against each other, in other words, those who accept God are against those who reject him, and those who reject him are against those who accept him. The language: *"A father will be divided against his son and a son against his father"* (*Luke* 12:53) emphasizes the radicalization of the divisions in the world.

Consequently, those who are for radical change set themselves in the direction of a head-on collision against those who protect the status quo. It is precisely through radical change that peace and unity are restored. And once that happens, fratricidal conflicts and confrontations will cease altogether. Christ Jesus expresses his deep desire to bring about unity and liberation to humankind: *"How great is my anguish until it is accomplished"* (*Luke* 12:50), and those who want to rescue humanity from division and self-destruction, experience the same anguish experienced by Jesus.

In the struggle for unity and equality, the survival of mankind is at stake

Who will survive? Those who are strong enough to live in unity, equality, and peace with all. Many *"will attempt to [survive] but will not be strong enough"* (*Luke* 13:24).

Why is it that many will not survive? Because many pursue their own wellbeing with disregard for the welfare of others, thus, establishing divisions within the human race. The possession of excessive riches and overwhelming power – dearly encouraged by our society –, frequently, confronts men against one another.

Living in a divided society becomes the final aim and goal for many who, overtly or subtly profess unconditional allegiance to worldly riches and power. And, so it happens, that those who promote division may in fact become the "first" in the world: *"Behold . . . some are first who will be last"* (*Luke* 13:30). They may be strong according to worldly standards, but will not be strong enough to follow the model of the communitarian God.

To be strong enough to survive requires a way of life in which: A) we live as children of God, and, B) we live on earth as if it were the beginning of our life in the Kingdom.

- A. Living as Children of God means living in accordance with our own nature, as people who have one Father; as people who share in the life of God. Living as children of God is fully realized only in the community of human beings where there is peace, unity, and equality among all, without exception.
- B. We begin to live in the Kingdom of God here on earth whenever we begin to rid ourselves of division and mutual exploitation; that is to say, whenever we strive at becoming well-rounded, complete persons. This is what makes us strong enough to survive.

4. Our humility ought to be the reflection of the humility we see in God

Humility is the way of life whereby a person makes himself equal to those who are treated as inferiors, so the highest level of human equality may be restored in all. In other words, the humble person restores equality by eradicating the inequalities between people in any area of human life. The humble person makes life to the fullest possible for everybody by sharing all he is and all he has with others. Humility defines what a person truly is.

Humility is a necessity of life: *"Humble yourself the more, the greater you are, and you will find favor with God"* (Sirach 3:18). That is, the greater a person, the more he strives to facilitate others to be what he is. By doing so, the humble person brings unity among the people with whom he relates: *"My son, conduct your affairs with humility, and you will be loved more than a giver of gifts"* (Sirach 3:17).

When God made himself man, he gave us the example of perfect humility because the one who is all goodness deemed it appropriate to make us equal to him. God is perfect humility, not so much for sharing with us what he has, but for sharing with us himself.

Our world is against humility

Those who hold worldly power set themselves apart from those who are weak, poor, afflicted or, in any way, seen as inferior. Those who lack humility abound in arrogance. To them, the strong are first, the weak are last; the wealthy are first, the poor are last. Therefore, worldly power is the opposite of humility, the antithesis of communitarian life.

Chapter XVII

HOW TO BUILD A PERMANENT HUMAN COMMUNITY. THE ROLE OF SOCIAL AND LABOR JUSTICE

It is man's aspiration to build a permanent human community because permanent is the unity of the trinitarian God. The durability of a community depends on men's ability to respect justice for all, especially socioeconomic justice of which labor justice is a crucial element. However, justice becomes fragile, or ceases to exist altogether, as a result of human actions leading to abuses, vengeance or exploitation of man by man.

1. It is necessary to avoid paying evil for evil

In order to build *common unity*, it is necessary to avoid paying evil for evil because such retribution causes harm to both the perpetrator and the victim:

- The perpetrator of a wrongdoing degrades his own human dignity by reason of his failure to respect the dignity of others.
- The victim of a wrongdoing is degraded because the harm, to which he is subjected, is an affront to his human dignity.

How to stop the spread of evil?

In the gospel of Matthew, Jesus gives the following explanation: *"If your brother sins [commits a wrong] against you, go and tell him his fault between you and him alone. If he listens to you, you have won over your brother"* (*Matthew* 18:15). It is in the hands of the victim (understood as an individual or a nation) to stop evil in its tracks, to correct its harmful effects by communicating with the wrongdoer in order to ask him to stop the wrongdoing. If he stops, evil no longer has control over the perpetrator; and will not produce ill effects on the victim either (for by refusing to resort to retaliation, the victim stops the vicious cycle of evil). In other words, evil has been defeated, and *"you have won over your brother."*

In order to stop the spread of evil, we must understand that we are all brothers (children of the same Father). And it is only when the victim of the wrongdoing fails to *go and tell [the perpetrator] of his fault* (so he may win over his brother) that evil takes over both of them … they have become enemies!

If a wrongdoer does not bring an end to his wrongdoing (*"does not listen"*), the victim – after exhausting all peaceful means available – is to treat the perpetrator as a *"Gentile or a tax collector"* (*Matthew* 18:17). Now, how did Christ Jesus treat "gentiles and tax collectors"? He gave his life to save them!

God warns us: *"If I tell the wicket man that he shall surely die, and you do not speak out to dissuade the wicket man from his way, he [the wicket man] shall die for his guilt, but I will hold you responsible for his death"* (*Ezekiel* 33:8-9).

Christ comes to the world to "tell" men of their wrongdoings (individually and collectively) so that, if they listen to him, *he has won over his brothers.* Through men of good will, Jesus continues to approach wrongdoers so he may win them over: *"Where two or more are gathered together in my name, there am I in the midst of them"* (*Matthew* 18:20). Christ is in the midst of those who gather together to win their brothers, to eradicate all forms of wrongdoing in the world. Whenever God is in the midst of two or more persons, they no longer harm one another; evil ceases to exist.

2. Forgiveness is a barrier against mutual destruction

There is something that prevents men from destroying one another, something that is necessary for building a durable community, something which ensures the survival of humankind: Forgiveness.

In Matthew's gospel, Jesus says that forgiveness is born out of compassion: *"Moved with compassion the master of that servant let him go and forgave him the loan" (Matthew* 18:27). Forgiveness is born out of compassion for a suffering humanity, for a humanity growing increasingly divided.

In the world today, societal disintegration is ignited and fueled by the conflicts between men, and the wrongs they inflict upon each other.

In order to prevent self-destruction, a person must:

-   Understand that everybody shares the same human dignity.
-   Understand that the wrong inflicted upon one is a wrong inflicted upon all.
-   Expect that the suffering of one person should move everyone else to compassion.

The one who forgives his offender reaffirms the expectation that the one who has been forgiven will, in turn, forgive others. If the one who is forgiven fails to forgive others, he will be responsible for breaking the unity among humans.

If we define forgiveness as the capacity to preserve unity among men, we must agree on the following:

-   Forgiveness is not merely a way of behaving; it is rather a way of life. That is to say, in order to live as a true human being, one must forgive others.
-   Forgiveness knows no limits, neither in quality nor quantity. *Is it enough to forgive seven times? "I say to you, not seven times, but seventy-seven times" (Matthew* 18:22); in other words, always!
-   Forgiveness does not end in a unilateral action; it is continued in all the interactions between men. This is why the one who is forgiven is expected, in turn, to forgive others.

- Forgiveness opens the doors to life; it is the never-ending source of life in human history.

Those who break the unity among men have lost their capacity to be *moved with compassion* in the face of the suffering of others. They have lost their capacity to forgive, to see themselves as members of humankind.

"Wrath and anger [war and destruction] are hateful things, yet [he who does not forgive] hugs them tight" (*Sirach* 27:30). Thus, it is necessary for us to *"set enmity aside; to remember death and decay"* (*Sirach* 28:6), and humanity will survive.

3. Labor justice, based on fair salaries, contributes to the prosperity of a lasting community

A fair salary is that which is in accordance with the worker's human dignity. In the gospel of Matthew, Jesus refers to the fair salary as the equal pay the "owner of a vineyard" gave to all his workers at the end of the day, even though some had worked longer than others. *"When those who had started about five o'clock came, each received the usual daily wage. So, when the first came, they thought that they would receive more, but each of them also got the usual wage"* (*Matthew* 20:9-10).

Why did the owner of the vineyard pay everybody the same wage? Because all men share the same human dignity, they all have the same human needs. Justice is served only when every person possesses what is required to meet his needs, at the highest level demanded by his human dignity – no more and no less.

God calls all people to acquire what they require to fully meet their needs

This call is issued to all: the owner of the vineyard went out to hire laborers *"at dawn . . . at about nine o'clock . . . around noon . . . around three o'clock . . . [and] about five o'clock."* The owner of the vineyard made every effort to ensure that no one is left *"standing here idle all day."* To all of them, he made the same call: *"you too go into my vineyard and I will give you what is just"* (*Matthew* 20:1-7).

The ones who oppose labor justice

They are the ones who *"grumbled against the landowner"* (*Matthew* 20:11), the ones who are opposed to human equality, the ones who place themselves "above" others, the ones who are enemies of the universal welfare of humanity, the ones who seek division among people, the ones who always want more than what they need. *"Thus, the last will be first and the first will be last"* (*Matthew* 20:16). To those who make themselves first, God says: *"My thoughts are not your thoughts, nor are your ways my ways . . . As high as the heavens are above the earth, so high are my ways above your ways and my thoughts above your thoughts"* (*Isaiah* 55:8-9).

Before God's eyes, labor justice is a means to:

A. Ensure that men earn what is necessary for them to meet their needs.
B. Respect the equality and unity among all.

True labor justice is realized when all men earn according to their need; that is to say, according to their human dignity.

4. The human community cannot be divided, otherwise, it may not survive

Just as the trinitarian God cannot be divided, so it is with the members of the human community. If we decide to live in *common unity*, we cannot leave anybody outside of it. If one of the Persons of the Trinity were to break up the unity, it will be the end of the trinitarian God because it is no longer one. Now, when we accept the Trinity in our life, we must accept it in its totality, without adding nor subtracting anything.

Inasmuch as Christ, the Second Person of the Trinity, revealed to us the totality of the trinitarian God, we are to believe in God totality, otherwise, we do not believe in God at all.

Christ offers himself to us totally. For instance, when he speaks to us we must hear all he has to say; when he gives us his life, we must take it all, nothing less, nothing more. We must receive from Christ all he has for us, or else we are not true believers in him.

What does Christ do for us?

- He brings us salvation, *"he comes to save you. Then will the eyes of the blind be opened, the ears of the deaf be cleared; then will the lame leap like a stag, then the tongue of the dumb will sing. Streams will burst forth in the desert, and rivers in the steppe. The burning sands will become pools"* (*Isaiah* 35:4-7).
- He *"secures justice for the oppressed, gives food to the hungry . . . sets prisoners free . . . gives sight to the blind . . . raises up those who are bowed down . . . protects the stranger, sustains the orphan and the widow"* (*Psalm* 146:7-9).
- He makes it possible for *"those who are poor in the world to be rich in faith and heirs of the Kingdom"* (*James* 2:5).
- He takes us (individually) *"away from the crowd"* (*Mark* 7:33) and opens our ears and removes the impediment from our speech so we may hear and speak the totality of what he wants us to hear and proclaim.

On the contrary, those who take from Christ only what is convenient for them, distort his truth in order to justify their own selfish interests. True unity with Christ, therefore, requires that we take him in his totality, without distorting or watering him down, without adjusting him in accordance with our worldly conveniences.

The stronger the unity between men, the more durable the community

Indeed, men's true task in life is to unify the community. However, some decide to divide it.

A. **Who unifies the community?** he who seeks the welfare of others before his own; he who seeks unity, equality, and respect for all through humble service; he who joins the oppressed in their struggle for liberation. Anyone who seeks unity between men, must take upon himself the suffering of being rejected, of being misunderstood, of being falsely accused, of being the victim of conspiracies, even of being put to death. Thus, *"whoever loses his life for my [Christ's] sake and that of the gospel will save it"* (*Mark* 8:35).

B. **Who divides the community?** He who lives to accumulate riches and power; he who looks after his own interests and wellbeing with disregard of other people. Thus, *saving one's life*, as understood by worldly standards, produces the opposite effect: *"whoever wishes to save his life will lose it"* (*Mark* 8:35).

Consequently, the more seriously men take their responsibility to live in community, the more permanent the latter will be.

Christ reveals himself so that we may join him in a community of life

Based of Christ own revelation of himself, men find it difficult to establish a community of life with him. Why? Because Christ says: *"'The Son of Man is to be handed over to men and they will kill him, and three days after his death he will rise.' But they did not understand the saying, and they were afraid to question him"* (*Mark* 9:31-32).

Why would men be afraid to ask for clarification as to the meaning of the above statement? Because if the powerful of the world kill the leader, they will also kill the followers. Therefore, it is better not to ask any questions and not to understand; it is better to ignore, to change the subject or, even, to dismiss the statement as unrealistic. For, after all, who would want to kill a good and righteous man?

History shows that the unjust of the world continue to kill good and righteous men.

Why does the world kill them? Because the unjust say: *"Let us beset the just one, because he is obnoxious to us; he sets himself against our doings, reproaches us for transgressions of the law and charges us with violation of our training"* (*Wisdom* 2:12).

In order to prevent the powerful of the world from separating us from Christ, we must look at the unity between him and his Father. The source of our strength lies in that unity, which *"is first of all, pure, then peaceable, gentle, compliant, full of mercy and good fruits, without inconstancy or insincerity." The wisdom of God "is sown in peace for those who cultivate in peace"* (*James* 3:17, 18). Therefore, the wisdom of God gives us the understanding we need in order to remove our fears to ask questions concerning the truth Christ reveals to us. Since that truth is always based on the unity between man and God, and the unity between men themselves, any division of men in antagonistic classes goes against the wisdom of God.

A divided society brings *"bitter jealousy and selfish ambition . . . disorder and every foul practice"* (*James* 3:14). Under these circumstances, men live in fear, the fear of living in a fractured society. The revelation Christ makes of himself, however, gives us the certainty that if we remain united with him, we can defeat the forces of division just as he defeated the forces of death.

The crucifixion and resurrection, Christ predicted for himself, are inseparable insofar as they are elements of a sequence, which projects the human community towards eternity. With his resurrection, Christ made it possible for man to be an integral part of the trinitarian God, just as Christ is part of the Trinity.

When Christ told his disciples that he would be crucified and *"three days after his death he would rise"*, he was including them in his own resurrection, and in the reunification with the trinitarian God in a permanent community.

Chapter XVIII

HUMAN ATTRIBUTES PROSPER IN A COMMUNITY. THE ADMINISTRATION OF MATERIAL GOODS

1. Three basic human attributes

*T*here are three basic human attributes, which prosper in the community namely, **unity, freedom and compassion.**

In the parable of the Prodigal Son, the evangelist Luke relates a family situation wherein one of the sons leaves his father's home and later returns (*Luke* 15:11-32). In order for us to present the human attributes indicated above, we will apply that family situation to society in general.

A. **Human unity** is best presented in the context of the relationship between a parent (father or mother) and a child. This relationship reflects the most intimate unity between two persons. The unity of the members of the family is the normal state (the essence) of the family, just as the normal state (essence) of humanity is realized in its members living in unity.

But once the son separates himself from the family, he alienates the nature of the family. Similarly, when human beings separate themselves from each other, human nature is alienated.

B. **Freedom.** In accordance with his freedom, the son decides to leave his family. The father, respectful of such a decision, does not interfere with his son's freedom. Human nature suffers as much harm when a family member is deprived of his freedom, as when any member of society is deprived of his freedom. It is a solid foundation of human nature that every person be free both within the family and within society at large.

C. **Compassion.** The father, as the head of a broken family, is fully aware of the damage his son has caused to the integrity of the family. In his compassion, the father values his son more than anything else, and wants him back so the unity of the family may be restored. The father's care and his genuine joy at the return of his son are of the essence to the family and to the entire human race.

Compassion is an integral element of human nature because without it, men would end up destroying themselves in acts of vengeance, prompted by the harm caused by one another. Without compassion, the father would have rejected his son's willingness to return, thus leaving the family permanently incomplete.

Nowadays, humanity finds itself in an "unnatural" state because of the unwillingness of humans to live in unity.

2. Human loyalty strives when men live in community

When men live in community, they enhance their ability to be loyal to everything in and around them just as God, the Creator and Redeemer, is loyal to everything he creates and redeems. Our life in community – the community wherein Christ also lives – allows us to be loyal to other persons, to ourselves, and to the material goods we need to sustain our lives.

A. Loyalty to other persons and to self

Our loyalty to Christ is the foundation of our loyalties to other persons, even to ourselves. *"If anyone comes to me without hating his father or mother, wife and children, brothers and sisters or even his own life, he cannot be my disciple"* (*Luke* 14:26). This statement does not mean that, in order for us to be loyal to Christ, we must disown our loved ones. On the contrary, it means that if we remain loyal to Christ, his redeeming power will enhance our loyalties to our loved ones and to everybody else, including ourselves.

We must keep in mind that there are very powerful commitments in our human relations that can lead us away from God. Regardless of how powerful a human relation may be (such as between a parent and child, a husband and wife, a citizen and his country, or a constituent and his political party), it cannot be opposed to, or diminish in any way our loyalty to God, because he perfects all loyalties.

B. Loyalty to material possessions

Our loyalty to Christ places our loyalty to material possessions in its proper dimension. *"Every one of you who does not renounce all his possessions cannot be my disciple"* (*Luke* 14:33). This does not mean that, in order to be loyal to Christ, a person is to deprive himself of the necessities required to sustain life. What it means is that people cannot subordinate themselves to material possessions. In fact, a person cannot place possessions above himself, above others, or above God.

Furthermore, it is only by being loyal to God that we will be capable of giving possessions their proper use, that is, the collective benefit of all humanity.

It goes without saying that, in a fragmented and materialistic world, being loyal to Christ is a tremendously demanding challenge because: *"Whoever does not carry his own cross and come after me cannot be my disciple"* (*Luke* 14:27). Here the term "cross" emphasizes the nature of the confrontation between Christ and the prevailing "world order," as well as the degree of difficulty confronted to remain loyal to God.

3. The administration of material goods

Depending of the way we administer material goods, we may fall under two categories: *"The children of light"* and *"the children of the world"* (*Luke* 16: 8).

- "The children of light" are those who place their trust in God, not in their material possessions and use them for the benefit of everybody.
- "The children of this world" are those who place their trust in their worldly possessions and use them only for their self-serving interests.

The proper use of material goods

A. Material goods are to be used only to meet our needs at the highest level required by our human dignity.
B. Material goods are not to be administered in a way that may result in their accumulation beyond what is necessary to meet our needs, lest said possessions become wealth (mammon) and, therefore, an outward sign of the appropriation of what belongs to all. (Wealth – accumulated possessions – becomes an injustice whenever there is even one single person whose needs have been left unmet). With wealth (mammon) comes greed, and with greed, oppression.

Who are those who accumulate wealth? (*Amos* 8:4-7):

- Those *"who trample upon the needy and destroy the poor of the land."*
- Those who fraudulently sell at the highest possible price, goods or services that have been reduced to the lowest possible quality. To sell their grain, they *"will diminish the ephah, add to the shekel, and fix [their] scales for cheating!"*
- Those who appropriate for themselves the larger portion of the worker's fair salary. They *"buy the lowly man for silver, and the poor man for a pair of sandals."*

Concerning those who serve mammon, God says: *"Never will I forget a thing they have done!"* (*Amos* 8:7).

In his First Letter to Timothy, Saint Paul writes that "the children of light" employ their material possessions, their talents, their creativity, and their ingenuity in devising means to spread the "light" to the world. They resort to the means of "light", such as dialogue, understanding, mutual respect. By doing so, they become administrators of peace and justice.

Furthermore, "the children of light" use effective means to turn "the children of this world" into "children of light." *"First of all, then, I ask that supplications, prayers, petitions, and thanksgivings be offered for everyone, for kings and for all in authority [the children of this world], that we may live a quiet and tranquil life in all devotion [justice] and dignity"* (*1 Timothy* 2:1-2).

The accumulation of wealth is an impediment to unity between men

Accumulated wealth is that which is not shared among all; it is the wealth a person keeps for himself beyond what is necessary for the satisfaction of his needs. It is the wealth a person cannot share with the poor; it is the wealth whose use is different than that given it by the Creator. In brief, accumulated wealth is that which is not used for the satisfaction of the needs of all.

In the gospel of Mark, Jesus tells the rich man: *"Go, sell what you have, and give it to the poor"* (*Mark* 10:21). This means "your" wealth belongs to those who need it. The wealth, which causes division among men, therefore, is that which is accumulated in a few hands. This wealth becomes so desirable to the rich man, that he cannot live without it; it becomes an addiction; it generates a dependency almost impossible to depart from. *"It is easier for a camel to pass through the eye of a needle than for one who is rich to enter the kingdom of God"* (*Mark* 10:25). Accumulated wealth indeed turns itself against the person who possesses it.

Wealth used as a means for unification

This wealth goes beyond the possession of material goods, and finds the reason for its existence in the satisfaction of the needs of all. In the scriptural passage cited above, if the rich man had sold his possessions and given them to the poor, he would have ended his worldly wealth and taken over the wealth of God; he would have removed the obstacle between him and God.

Administering the wealth that unifies men is a way of life consisting in the caring and harmonious relationships between people. This wealth does not lead us to take possession over other persons; on the contrary, it allows us to respect each other as members of a unified humanity. Referring to this wealth, Jesus says: *"There is no one who has given up house or brothers or sisters or mother or father or children or lands for my sake and for the sake of the gospel, who will not receive a hundred times more now in this present age: houses and brothers and sisters and mothers and children and lands"* (*Mark* 10:29-30).

In other words, once we place our material possession and our family relationships in the hands of God, we gain more possessions than what we gave up, and experience the joy of relating to all human beings as if they were our mother or our father or our children.

4. Greed for wealth is a trap to the rich

Saint Luke in his gospel describes a situation where a rich man falls into the trap of his own wealth… and was never able to get out of it. *"There was a rich man who dressed in purple garments and fine linen and dined sumptuously each day. And lying at his door was a poor man named Lazarus, covered with sores, who would gladly have eaten his fill of the scraps that fell from the rich man's table"* (*Luke* 16: 19-21).

What causes "the rich man" to fall into the trap of his own wealth?

A. The self-gratification he receives from his wealth. The rich man "dressed in purple garments and fine linen dined sumptuously each day". His "good" life renders him unwilling to acknowledge the needs of the one who is in misfortune. His wealth numbs his sensitivity toward the needs of others.

B. The indifference, insensitivity, and total disregard for the suffering of someone who is right next to him, of someone he knows. Even though, the poor man "is at his [the rich man's] door," he just does not care; he behaves as if he has lost the notion of what the human family is.

C. The illusory expectation that he can enjoy his wealth forever. In other words, the enjoyment the rich man receives from his wealth prevents him from coming to grips with his own mortality, with the temporality of his life. Each day he dresses superbly and dines sumptuously. But apparently, he is not aware of the passing of his days; he believes that his "good" life, his "good" days will never end.

The transgression of the rich man consists of two elements:

A. His indifference toward the suffering of others and,

B. His inability to utilize his wealth to meet the needs of others.

By his indifference, he separates himself from the human family. And, by his inability to utilize his wealth to meet the needs of the poor, he distorts the purpose for which material possessions exist – the satisfaction of the needs of all. Thus, the rich man assigns to himself the exclusive "right" to use material goods for his own benefit.

The rich also present themselves collectively as a group: *"Woe to the complacent [those who feel secure in their riches] . . . Lying upon beds of ivory, stretched comfortably on their couches . . . They drink wine from bowls and anoint themselves with the best oils; yet they are not made ill by the fall of [the nation]. Therefore, now they shall be the first ones to go into exile, and their wanton revelry shall be done away with"* (*Amos* 6: 1, 4-7). The rich show callous disregard for the tragedies and sufferings afflicting entire nations. The rich and powerful are members of a socioeconomic class maintaining antagonistic relations with the members of the poor and disenfranchised classes.

How can the rich man break free from his trap?

He can get free from his trap by laying *"hold of eternal life,"* and by pursuing *"righteousness, devotion, faith, love, patience"* and compassion before human suffering (*1 Timothy* 6:11-12).

5. The concurrence of man's will and God's will is necessary to appropriately administer material goods

In order to properly administer material possessions, the will of God and the will of man must converge in one heart. To do the will of God means to listen, to think, and to act like he does. He makes himself one of us so his will and our will may be one; in other words, when we do the will of Christ, we do the will that is already within our very selves. The Lord says to us, *"Go out and work in the vineyard today"* (*Matthew* 21:28), for there is nothing in God's will that could ever be harmful or detrimental to us.

We are able to join in the will of God whenever we, human beings, are *"of the same mind, with the same love, united in heart, thinking one thing,"* united in spirit and ideals, doing *"nothing out of selfishness or out of vainglory; rather, humbly regarding others as more important than [ourselves], each looking out not for his own interests, but everyone for those of others"* (*Philippians* 2:2-4).

Each person must develop the ability to do the will of his fellow human beings in order to reach unity among all, and taking the will of God as a model, which is always good, compassionate, self-giving, and just. *"Have among yourselves the same attitude that is also yours in Christ Jesus"* (*Philippians* 2:5).

It is by doing the will of God that our will becomes one with the will of God, our hearts become one with the heart of Christ Jesus.

Destructive actions are the result of the break-up of the unity between the will of God and the will of man.

Whenever men fail to establish a common unity among themselves, they also fail to establish a common unity with the Almighty. And this is a cause of destructive conflicts in the world. The following is a description of the destruction resulting from the collision of antagonistic wills: *"When vintage time drew near [the owner of the vineyard] sent his servants to the tenants to obtain his product. But the tenants seized the servants and one they beat, another they killed, and a third they stoned. Again he sent other servants, more numerous than the first ones, but they treated them in the same way. Finally, he sent his son to them… [but they] killed him" (Matthew 21:34-39).*

Applying this parable to life in society, the tenants are the people who have been given the task of administering the vineyard of humanity so that it may produce fruits of unity and life. When the tenants fail to live up to such a task, God sends his people to restore compliance with his will. But the tenants respond by seizing and killing the people of God, thus, unleashing the horrors of killing.

When do "the tenants" of our world unleash the horrors of killing?

- Whenever they deprive others of what they need.
- Whenever they deprive others of their right to life.
- Whenever they use the economic resources for purposes other than the satisfaction of human needs.
- Whenever they spread half-truths in order to justify a state of oppression.

The vineyard *"will be taken away from [them] and given to a people who will make it produce its fruit" (Matthew 21:43).* God builds his "vineyard" (our world) to be a place of peace, justice and unity: *"What more was there to do for my vineyard that I had not done?" (Isaiah 5:4).* God *"looked for judgment, but see, bloodshed! For justice, but hark, the outcry!" (Isaiah 5:7).* The new administrators of the vineyard of humanity must turn it into a place where the horrors of killing are no more. *"Then the God of peace will be with you" (Philippians 4:9).*

Living in unity with God is like enjoying a banquet

Unity between men and God is like a "banquet of life" because unity always generates life and abundance and joy: *"Behold, I have prepared my banquet, my calves and fattened cattle are killed, and everything is ready" (Matthew 22:4).* This "banquet" is the joyful realization of all human aspirations: *"the Lord God will wipe away the tears from all faces"; "he will destroy death forever" (Isaiah 25:8);* it is a banquet to which everyone is invited… especially Lazarus.

However, there are some who reject the invitation because they cannot tolerate a universal human order based on unity and equality. This order is not acceptable, convenient, or desirable to them; in fact, it is detrimental to their interests.

Furthermore, the "banquet of life" is a threat to those who are not interested in the well-being of humanity; so much a threat that they *"ignored the invitation and went away, one to his farm, another to his business" (Matthew* 22:5). The invitation to the "banquet" represented such a serious threat that those who rejected the invitation *"laid hold of [the Lord's] servants, mistreated them, and kill them" (Matthew* 22:6). Nowadays, those who promote inequality and oppression will do the same to anyone who *invites* them to establish unity and equality in the world.

A "wedding garment" is required

All that is required to enter the banquet is a commitment to purse the wellbeing of all, the liberation of all, and to identify oneself with all that Christ stands for. In other words, this requirement consists in taking the identity of Christ because he is the appropriate *wedding garment*. He who came into the banquet not dressed in a wedding garment was *"cast into the darkness outside" (Matthew* 22:13), the darkness of the absence of the God of unity, the darkness of ongoing inequality and oppression.

Who are those who accept the invitation to the banquet of unity?

- Those who see God in every human being (especially in Lazarus)
- Those who seek the welfare of others.
- Those who denounce and oppose all forms of oppression and exploitation of man by man (*Mark* 9:38).
- Those who help anyone in need because he belongs to Christ (*Mark* 9:41).

In brief, treating others as God would treat us is the equivalent of accepting God's invitation to unity.

What is the main reason to reject the invitation to the banquet of unity?

The accumulation of wealth! Those whose ultimate purpose in life is the accumulation of wealth, for their own selfish interests, have no other recourse but to reject the invitation. The apostle James, in his Letter, identifies them as: **the *rich*** (*James* 5:1), to whom other human beings are but mere "tools" to make wealth.

Let us indicate that wealth in itself is neutral, neither good nor bad. It becomes good or bad depending on the modality by which it is acquired and used. The material wealth produced and utilized for the satisfaction of our needs – even at the highest level required by our human dignity – does not constitute wealth.

According to James, people become rich by the manner in which they acquire wealth, and by the manner in which they use it.

- **The manner in which they acquire wealth.** They acquire wealth by withholding the wages *"from the workers who harvested [their] fields... and the cries of the harvesters have reached the ears of the Lord of hosts"* (*James* 5:4).
- **The manner in which they use wealth.** The rich use wealth in two ways:

  A. They use it only for themselves: *"You have lived on earth in luxury and pleasure; you have fattened your hearts for the day of slaughter"* (*James* 5:5).

  B. They use it as a means of domination: *"You have condemned; you have murdered the righteous one; he offers you no resistance"* (*James* 5:6).

Chapter XIX

ANTAGONISMS VS HARMONY WITHIN THE INSTITUTIONS OF SOCIETY

1. Antagonisms within society's institutions

*T*here are many antagonisms in the world's societal institutions. Here are some of those antagonisms:

- Within the economic institutions. There are conflicts between employer and laborer: the former wants to pay low wages, the latter wants fair salaries. The workers demand the right to organize themselves in labor unions, the employers oppose labor unions. The workers demand decent health care and retirement benefits, employers claim the increase in the cost of production is detrimental to their profits. There is antagonism between seller and buyer: one wants to charge high prices, the other wants affordable prices.
- Within the political institutions. There is conflict between the rulers and the people: the rulers protect their own interests and make promises they do not intend to fulfill; the people want responsible representatives and truthfulness in political commitments.

- In the area of international relations. There are conflicts between the nations of the world. Powerful nations want to expand their domination; weaker nations want to maintain their sovereignty.
- In family life. There are conflicts which harm the unity between the members of the family, conflicts with devastating consequences for the general society.

2. Is it possible to restore the harmony intended by God?

The situation in the world today indicates that we are dealing with a very difficult task. Those who believe that it is impossible to achieve harmony do so because they refuse to recognize that men have the capacity to return to the order instituted by God since the beginning of time. Others are convinced that harmony only exist in the minds and imagination of children who know nothing about the "real world." However, that is precisely what the world does not understand: *"Whoever does not accept the kingdom of God like a child will not enter it"* (*Mark* 10:15).

God has the power to restore harmony within the institutions of society

Inasmuch as the existence of antagonism, among men, is a social anomaly, the restoration of harmony to a society is as necessary as the restoration of good health to a sick person. Social harmony can be defined as the concordance between people's actions and the realization of the common good.

Christ's miraculous deeds on earth were intended to allow men to see God's power to cure all sorts of illnesses both individual and collective. Luke relates Jesus' miracle of the cure of ten lepers – a small collectivity of ill people. *"Ten were cleansed, were they not? Where are the other nine?"* (*Luke* 17:17), asked Jesus.

Of the ten who were cured, only one came back *"glorifying God in a loud voice"* (*Luke* 17:15), he was the only one of the ten who wanted to place his restored health in the hands of God and continue God's healing work, both individually and collectively. The one who returned was able to understand that he had established a relationship with God, and that the next step was to reestablish a relationship with his fellow human beings, relationship, which had been previously alienated by the illness of leprosy.

After a person is restored to good health, it is appropriate for him to say: I, your servant, *"will no longer offer holocaust or sacrifice to any other god except to the Lord"* (*2 Kings* 5:17).

The nations of the world will not cure their illnesses unless they return to God; in other words, unless we relate to one another as God relates to us. Humanity becomes healthy when men are capable of eradicating the antagonisms from the institutions of society.

This is how Christ becomes active in society's institutions: by turning death into life, illness into health, injustice into justice, and fragmentation into unity. Once God restores our wellbeing, *"we shall also live with him"* (*2 Timothy* 2:11). Just as the Redeemer cures the world from its societal maladies so must we collaborate with him by placing ourselves at the service of all.

Those who place their health, possessions, and talents at the service of mankind will hear the voice of God telling them: *"stand up and go; your faith has saved you"* (*Luke* 17:19).

Harmony between the institutions of society is an expression of our faith in God

To have faith in God means to believe that the power that is in him is also in us. In other words, it means that what he can do, we can also do.

What is the power of God we make ours through faith in him? The power of God is the power to forgive those who offend him, the power to bless those who curse him, the power to heal the wounded, the power to free the oppressed, the power to restore justice to the victims of injustice, and the power to give life to the dead.

The power of God is accessible to all men through faith, so that *"if you have faith the size of a mustard seed, you would say to this mulberry tree, 'Be uprooted and planted in the sea' and it would obey you"* (*Luke* 17:6).

These words are said in order to leave no doubt, whatsoever, about the absolute power of faith. However, is it not true that, in spite of the faith we claim to have, we still live in world afflicted by social antagonisms?

Aware of our own lack of faith, it becomes necessary for us to ask God: *"Increase our faith"* (*Luke* 17:5) so that we may share in his power and effectively participate in his work. It is the quality and degree of our commitment to faith in God that determines the extent of our participation in his power and the extent of our collaboration in his work.

Our faith in God must spread like a flame

"I remind you to stir into flame the gift of God that you have" (*2 Timothy* 1:6). We must spread – like a flame – the power to forgive our enemies, to bless those who curse us, and to bring new life to a world afflicted by injustice and oppression. *"For God did not give us a spirit or cowardice but rather of power and love and self-control"* (*2 Timothy* 1:7).

Harmony between men is inclusive not exclusive

Our relationship with Christ Jesus gives us the strength necessary to bring harmony to the institutions we create in society because it is proper of the Almighty to draw everything to himself, without excluding anything nor anybody. This unifying power also belongs to those who, willingly and without coercion, receive the God incarnate.

Here is the manner in which God draws men to himself: The Almighty respects men's freedom, and does not force his power on anybody. Consequently, man, as receptor of that power, must also use it in the same manner: seeking harmony without imposition because respect brings about unity, and imposition generates rejection.

In his gospel, Matthew speaks of a specific case in which Christ reaffirms harmony as an essential element for unity between political and religious institutions. Just like God created men to live in harmony so do men ought to create the institutions of society as sources of harmony. There are, however, attempts to create division between God and man, as well as division between the institutions man establishes in society. There is one question, which seems to summarize the attempts to create division: *"Is it lawful to pay the census tax to Caesar or not?"* (*Matthew* 22:17).

The answer: *"Repay to Caesar what belongs to Caesar and to God what belongs to God"* (*Matthew* 22:21) reaffirms that there is no division, or conflict, between man and God because they both are united in the common purse of the wellbeing for the entire human race – in every aspect of life. Therefore, all institutions of human society must be expressions of men's efforts to achieve unity and harmony between themselves, efforts that are also expressions of the will of God. For instance:

-   Scientific and technological institutions find their true purpose only when their achievements are placed at the service of all (not just of a few, lest science and technology become a source of division and conflict).
-   Economic institutions find their true purpose only when they produce and distribute the economic wealth for the benefit of all (not just for the benefit of a few, lest economic institutions become a source of dispossession).
-   Political institutions find their true purpose only when the sole objective of government is the welfare of all people (not just a few, lest political institutions become a source of oppression).
-   Religious institutions find their true purpose only when they pursue man's wellbeing in body and soul (not just in soul, lest religious institutions become disconnected from the will of God).

Therefore, the unifying element of all human institutions is their common goal: the wellbeing of all.

Is there a separation between Church and State?

If we accept that the common goal of all human institutions is the realization of the common good, we must conclude that Church and State, as social institutions, are united by the same goal, and differentiated by their specific perspectives: the religious and the political, respectively.

3. Love of neighbor is a source of harmony between the institutions of society

"You shall love your neighbor as yourself" (*Matthew* 22:39). Love of neighbor is a way of life that moves a person to do everything in his power for the wellbeing of others. Every time a person looks after the interests of others before his own interests, he is embarking on the pursuit of unity, peace, and justice for all. It is this meaning, which defines love as the summation of all human laws, of all human aspirations, of all human institutions. This is the love that the powers of the world find to be extremely dangerous to their existence.

Love of neighbor stands in frank opposition to the worldly powers of division, conflict, and injustice. Nevertheless, the world has found a way to "neutralize" the commandment of love by allowing it to continue to exist, but with a meaning that is totally distorted (which is an effective way of eliminating it). Thus, nowadays, the word "love" has been reduced to mean anything from an act of sexual intercourse to a prudish sentimental affection for something or someone, and voided of anything beneficial to humanity. As a result, the commandment of "love" has been turned into something totally alien to what God intended it to be.

Once "love" is stripped of its gospel meaning, some people can say that they abide by the commandment of love, while at the same time:

– Promote or support wars,
– Promote or encourage discrimination among ethnic groups,
– Promote or actively engage in the dispossession and impoverishment of others.

Service, as an expression of love, is a source of harmony between social classes. *"The greatest among you must be your servant"* (*Matthew* 23:11). Christ reveals himself as a servant to all, and, by being a servant, he attracts everyone to himself. Behold Christ, the servant:

– Christ's highest place of honor is the lowest place among humans.
– There is no burden carried by men that Christ has not carried himself.

- Everything Christ does is for the wellbeing of humanity.
- Christ's love for humankind is expressed through deeds, not through empty words.
- Christ opens the doors of prosperity to all people, not to just a privileged group.
- He instructs all men in the truth by removing the blindfold that prevents them from seeing clearly.
- God becomes a man because he honors human beings above everything else in creation, because he created men to be the highest dignity in creation. In the eyes of God, nothing else can have preeminence over a human being.
- The Redeemer will always remain faithful to his commitment to men, regardless of what their failures may be.
- God took human flesh so that he may be present in all.
- Christ offers himself in the most unselfish way, in the fullness of his will, without conditions so all human beings may freely receive him.
- God walks along men through history, pouring his prosperity and his justice over them, guiding them toward his glorious kingdom, a kingdom that begins here on earth.

Christ is the servant from whom we learn to be like him because he is our *teacher and savior* (*Matthew* 23:8-10).

4. The dominant classes are detrimental to harmony within society

In the gospel of Mark, Jesus speaks about the role of the dominant class in society: *"Those who are recognized as rulers over the [people] lord it over them, and their great ones make their authority over them felt"* (*Mark* 10:42). That is to say, the rulers of the world use their authority as a means to subjugate other human beings. The courageous confrontation against these rulers is the "cup" of sacrifice and the "baptism" of fire (*Mark* 10:39) to be received by those who engage in the efforts to restore harmony between antagonistic social classes.

What must we do in order to drink this "cup" and be "baptized" in this baptism?

A. We must be able to understand the reality of our world, a world of "rulers" who subjugate people, of "great ones" who oppress nations. We need to understand how damaging and, at the same time, how real are the relations based on dominance and oppression.

B. We must be willing to become servants to all because *"whoever wishes to be great among you will be your servant; whoever wishes to be first among you will be the slave of all"* (*Mark* 10:43-44). Throughout the history of world civilizations, the term *"servant"* designates a person who attends to someone else's needs. And the term "slave" refers to a person belonging to the lowest level of the socioeconomic system based on slavery, such as the one prevailing in the Roman Empire. In the context of the New Testament, the terms "servant" and "slave" have a meaning opposite to accumulation of wealth and concentration of power.

5. Does Christ listen to those who need help to restore harmony between social classes?

Yes! Mark's gospel writes about the case of a man who cries out to Christ for help. *"Bartimaeus, a blind man… on hearing that it was Jesus of Nazareth, he began to cry out and say, 'Jesus, son of David, have pity on me.' And many rebuked him, telling him to be silent. But he kept calling out all the more, 'Son of David, have pity on me.' Jesus stopped and said, 'Call him.' So they called the blind man, saying to him, 'Take courage; get up, he is calling you'. He threw aside his cloak, sprang up, and came to Jesus. Jesus said to him in reply, 'What do you want me to do for you?' The blind man replied to him, 'Master, I want to see'. Christ told him, 'Go your way; your faith has saved you.' Immediately he received his sight and followed him on the way"* (*Mark* 10:46-52).

Here is how we can call Christ's attention so that he may listen to our petitions for harmony in a world blinded by societal antagonisms:

- By crying out to him when he passes in front of us (*Mark* 10:47). We cry out to him because he is expecting us to call him; he wants to hear our voices because he knows we need him, and no one will be able to make us stop crying out to him.
- By keeping in mind that Christ will call us through the mediation of our brothers. "*Call him over,*" Christ says. And our brothers, in turn, tell us, "*Take courage, get up, he is calling you*" (*Mark* 10:49).
- By hurrying up to get close to him. Like the blind man, who "*threw aside his cloak, sprang up and came to Jesus*" (*Mark* 10:50), we too must throw aside anything that prevents us from springing up toward Christ.
- By receiving the power of seeing men with the eyes of Christ. Consequently, we will see people in need of sight, of unity, of harmony.
- By having the courage to follow Christ along the way to restoration of the true human community.

Love of neighbor is applicable both at the individual level and at the social level

Love of neighbor and love of God are inseparable and go hand in hand: "*You shall love the Lord your God with all your heart, with all your soul, with all your mind, and with all your strength . . . [and] you shall love your neighbor as yourself*" (*Mark* 12:30-31).

Love of neighbor has an individual dimension and a collective dimension. Just as the deeds of an individual are the means to demonstrate his love for his neighbor, so are the deeds of social institutions the means to demonstrate their love for the entire collectivity. In other words, a social institution is the collectively organized way to demonstrate our love of neighbor. All institutions of collective human life are to be the means by which man realizes his love for his neighbor. The social, political, economic, religious, cultural, scientific, technological, and all other institutions in the human collectivity are to be the vehicles for man to materialize his love for his neighbor.

Just as love of God establishes a harmonic relationship between us and God, so does love of neighbor establish a harmonic relationship between us and our fellow human beings. Why? Because the love God has for us becomes the model of the love we have for our neighbor. Consequently, to say *"You shall love your neighbor as yourself"* (*Mark* 12:31) means that the love man receives from God, is the same love man gives to all other men. Moreover, man truly loves himself only when the love of God is within him, in his heart, in his soul, and in his mind. (If the love of God is not within man, man's love for himself is only egotism and selfishness). Thus, whenever the love of God is in man, he is able to love his neighbor with the same love he has for himself.

The dominant classes try to exempt themselves from the unity of the one love "man-neighbor-God" in the following ways:

– By alleging that the "man-God" unity is different than the "man-neighbor" unity. The resulting situation is one where the members of the powerful classes may claim they love God, while harming their neighbor.

– By alleging that their private life is disconnected from their public life. The resulting situation is one where leaders and rulers may consider themselves God-loving individuals in their private life, while in their public life they promote wars, legalize racial discrimination, pass laws that make the poor poorer and the rich richer, etc.

– By alleging that the connection "man-God-neighbor" is strictly a religious issue, with no validity in any other institution of societal life (social, economic, political, military, judicial, etc.). The resulting situation is one whereby the powerful expel God from most areas of human society.

Chapter XX

JUSTICE IN THE COMMUNITY LEADS TO GOD

1. *"God... will see to it that justice is done for them speedily"* (Luke 18:8)

$\mathcal{T}$he pursuit of communitarian justice is the manner in which men walk towards God. The pursuit of justice involves a process consisting of the following steps:

A. Knowledge of our human nature. The process begins with an understanding of our human nature; that is, with the knowledge of who we are. We are God's *"chosen ones"* (*Luke* 18:7), children of God, and, as such, we are called to live in unity, peace, mutual respect, and harmony with one another. We are called to live as people who share equally everything we are and everything we have.

B. Awareness of a loss. We must be conscious of the fact that, by our own divisive and destructive actions, we have lost our condition of being the chosen ones of God, and have become incomplete individuals separated not only from our fellow human being, but also from God.

C. Awareness of the need to restore what we have lost, to restore our wholeness. To better describe this awareness, the evangelist Luke presents the following analogy: In a town, there was a widow who, in the awareness of her weakness and need, persistently and tirelessly claimed before a judge, her right to justice; and justice was granted to her (*Luke* 18:1-5). The poor, the weak, the suffering, the oppressed, and the powerless must persistently claim their right to justice, to regain what was lost. We must be *"persistent whether it is convenient or inconvenient"* (*2 Timothy* 4:2).

D. Commitment to fight for justice in unity with God, who has become one of us by taking on our human nature so he may be in us, and us in him. Therefore, since God is already in our midst, our commitment to justice is also God's commitment.

Our fight for justice is not only a human action, but also the action of God who lives in us. Therefore, we *must "remain faithful to what [we] have learned and believe… so that one who belongs to God may be competent, equipped for every good work"* (*2 Timothy* 3:14,17).

2. A righteous man practices justice

Who is righteous?

Righteous is the one who *"hears the cry of the oppressed. He is not deaf to the wail of the orphan, nor to the widow when she pours out her complaint"* (*Sirach* 35:13, 14). Righteousness is a way of life, which consists of our total commitment to serve our fellow human beings, especially those who are afflicted by adversity or injustice. The righteous person is concerned with the welfare of others, not his own; he is not motivated by public praise, but by the love of God, who lives in him and in every person. The righteous person is aware of his own limitations and the effectiveness of the service he offers to his fellowmen; he is always in front of God, the source of his strength.

The one who lacks righteousness, on the other hand, sees his own wellbeing as more important than anybody else's. The people who lack righteousness find themselves in need of creating their own standard of righteousness, which is imposed on the rest of society. In this manner, those who lack righteousness become the model of "virtue" for the people, they place themselves above all others, and claim that they are *"not like the rest of humanity – greedy, dishonest, adulterous"* (*Luke* 18:11).

Those who possess worldly power and those who accumulate wealth for themselves, usually present themselves as being righteous before the eyes of the people, even though they lack righteousness. The one who *"despises everyone else"* (*Luke* 18:9) or is indifferent to the needs of others, and is still convinced of his own righteousness, is convinced only of a great lie. He believes he is "right"; he believes he represents the goal of humanity; he proclaims he is the model for everybody to follow and imitate.

The righteous person, on the other hand, lives in the presence of a God who humbled himself and is forever exalted: *"everyone who exalts himself will be humbled, and the one who humbles himself will be exalted"* (*Luke* 18:14). By becoming the servant of all, Christ humiliated himself in order to exalt the human race. Now, we are to follow the example of Christ by becoming the servants of all so he may exalt those who serve, those who are truly righteous.

Once we achieve righteousness, we must not let it go

Christ Jesus, the righteous man *par excellence*, asks us to receive him in our homes: *"Today I must stay in your house"* (*Luke* 19:5) because he wants to bring his presence (a presence of righteousness) into the home of humanity.

Christ's proposition receives two responses from us:

A. A response of acceptance: *"Behold, half of my possessions, Lord, I shall give to the poor, and if I have extorted anything from anyone, I shall repay it four times over"* (*Luke* 19:8). This answer is a way of saying that righteousness has entered in our house: *"salvation has come to this house"* (*Luke* 19:9). This is the reason Christ comes to the world.

B. A response of rejection: a response from those who *"began to grumble, saying, 'He has gone to stay at the house of a sinner'"* (*Luke* 19:7). Those who are entrenched in their unjust ways have already established their own "order" (of division and injustice); they reject anybody who brings equality, unity, and justice; they are interested in imposing their dominion, and, in order to do so, they are compelled to create a state ("a house") of deception and lies.

The unjust man believes he does not need to receive Christ

Those who are unjust seek to stay away from Christ, lest they be invited to live in unity and justice with all. Unjust men do not want to give Jesus the opportunity to say to them: *"today I must stay in your house."* However, in spite of being rejected by the unjust, Christ always remains committed to seeking those who are lost; he continues to tell everybody: *"today I must stay in your house"* (*Luke* 19:5).

3. Wisdom leads us to justice

Wisdom begins with the recognition of the supreme value of human life, and it reaches its perfection with the unwavering commitment to respect it. A person of wisdom is, therefore, someone who is *"awake"* to receive the Lord of life (*Matthew* 25:13). (Just like five *wise virgins*, who waited in the night for the coming of the bridegroom, were in possession of enough oil to keep their lamps burning).

Since every person is endowed with life, everyone has the responsibility and the right to respect it, both individually and collectively, under any state or condition. Insofar as respect for life is the foundation of true wisdom, the "wise" are those who make sure life is nurtured and fulfilled in every person without exception. In his gospel, Matthew presents five *"wise virgins"* as the embodiment of wisdom because they demonstrated respect for their own life and the life of others. (For this reason, they brought additional oil with them to ensure that nothing would prevent them from receiving the *"bridegroom"*, that is, the Lord of life).

The *"foolish virgins"*, on the other hand, showed no respect for their own life or the life of others. The foolish make no provision to ensure that life is respected or protected, because they truly do not care about human life (Just like the five foolish virgins did not care about bringing extra oil for their lamps). The foolish are satisfied with life for the *moment*, but do not care about all the dimensions of life.

Wisdom is much more than just knowledge or expertise. Wisdom involves the ability to live in unity with other human beings and with God, who is the source and fountain of life itself.

Justice among men. True human justice is not determined by the possessions a man has, but by man's capacity to utilize his possessions for the benefit of all mankind.

The following is an illustration of how human justice works: *"a man, who was going on a journey, called in his servants and entrusted his possessions to them. To one he gave five talents; to another, two; to a third, one – to each according to his ability"* (Matthew 25:14-15). The fact that each received talents is the beginning of human justice, notwithstanding the difference in the amounts received.

Who perseveres in human justice and who does not?

A. Those who multiplied their talents for the welfare of humanity persevered in human justice: *"The one who had received five talents came forward bringing the additional five. He said, 'Master you gave five talents. See I have made five more' . . . Then the one who had received two talents also came forward and said, 'Master, you gave two talents. See, I have made two more'"* (Matthew 25:20-22). In the eyes of the master, both servants contributed to prosperity and both received the same response: *"Well done, my good and faithful servant . . . Come share your master's joy"* (Matthew 25:21-22).

Justice among men is, therefore, the product of having contributed, with all of one's potential, to the benefit of mankind (each one contributed with everything they had).

B. He who fails to contribute to the welfare of humanity hinders human justice because he fails to produce what is needed for the benefit of his fellowmen. He is interested only in himself and refuses to work for the benefit of others. The unjust one *buried the talent he had received* (*Matthew* 25:18), and separated himself from his fellow human beings by refusing to seek their welfare. Consequently, he will be thrown out as a *"useless servant into the darkness outside, where there will be wailing and grinding of teeth"* (*Matthew* 25:30).

Any person (or nation) who does not follow justice will eventually end up harming himself. A society built on injustice can only sustain itself through a false "order", whereby men proclaim that they live in *"peace and security"* only to see that *"sudden disaster comes upon them, . . . and they will not escape"* (*1 Thessalonians* 5:3).

Human justice is God's design. Those who take on the responsibility of maintaining and promoting human justice through the use of their earthly possessions and their talents (the use of "small matters"), will share in "great responsibilities": the "Master's joy", and a world where justice prevails.

Economic injustice harms humankind

Economic injustice appears when a person (or a group) accumulates material goods beyond what is required for the satisfaction of needs. This injustice is prone to spread itself uncontrollably because the ambition to accumulate wealth has no limits, whereas the satisfaction of human needs does. It is for this reason that Christ says to the rich man: *"Go, sell what you have, and give it to the poor and you will have treasure in heaven"* (Mark 10:21). The difficulties of sharing accumulated wealth are overwhelming because the rich man becomes addicted to his wealth, and cannot separate himself from it.

On the other hand, let us observed that in the parable of the talents, the man who received five talents earned five more, and the one who received two earned two more... but neither one of them accumulated his wealth; on the contrary, they gave it to their master (who in this parable represents the communitarian God) for the benefit of the community.

4. How grave are the injustices afflicting humanity?

The gospel of Mark uses a symbolic language to describe the gravity of the injustices afflicting humanity. In a world where men suffer the tribulations of war, aggression, oppression, injustice, and selfishness, we can say symbolically that men are living under *a darkened sun, darkened moon, disintegrating stars, or shaken heavenly powers* (*Mark* 13:25-26).

The resolution of the injustices

In the same way the sun is supposed to give light, not darkness, so is man to promote unity, not division. In the same way the moon is to reflect the light, every man is to reflect the goodness of his heart by sharing in the wealth of the earth. In the same way the stars are to be permanent in the firmament, so are the achievements of man to be used for the common good of all mankind. In the same way the powers of heaven are the immutable foundation of life, so is man to seek life, not death.

Who will resolve the injustices? Everyone with the vocation to do it! God will *"gather his elect from the four winds, from the end of the earth to the end of the sky"* (*Mark* 13:27). The elect are those who bring justice to the world, those to whom God gives his *"great power and glory"* (*Mark* 13:26) to assist them in eradicating all forms of injustice.

When will this happen?

As a victim or witness of the injustices in the world, man knows what to do in order to bring injustice to an end (or, at least, he wishes it to come to an end). But of that day or hour, *no one knows... but only the Father.* (*Mark* 13:32). And, when the fullness of the trinitarian God comes to dwell in man, he will know the Father's will.

The *children of God* will overcome the injustices of the world

In the gospel of Luke, Jesus uses the expression *"children of God"* to describe those who are in unity with God (*Luke* 21:36). The children of God overcome the injustices of the world and *"are deemed worthy to attain to the coming age and to the resurrection of the dead"* (*Luke* 21:35).

What are the injustices of the world? They are the inequalities and divisions preventing people from living as children of God. Indeed, our world (*this age*) promotes division over unity; brute force over rational deliberation; abuse over respect; and deceit over trustworthiness. Those who perpetuate *this age* of injustice and division do not believe in and do not expect to live beyond this world, for they make themselves unworthy *"to attain to the coming age and to the resurrection of the dead."* They refuse to live as children of God, they lack life within themselves, and cannot continue living into the coming age.

How do we overcome the injustices of the present world? By living in unity with one another, as members of one universal community, as children of God. And, *"the children of God . . . are the ones who will rise"* (*Luke* 20: 36).

5. A world without justice is like a temple without God

God is in our midst in order *"to govern the world with justice and the peoples with fairness"* (*Psalm* 98:9). God is in our midst because we are his temple, the temple we take care of by living in justice. However, if our injustices damage the temple, Christ comes to restore justice within us, justice within his temple.

A nation that respects justice is like a temple where God lives; that nation will survive, inasmuch as justice is the means to ensure peaceful living among its people. Justice is a way of life whereby men relate to one another in accordance with what they are; that is, as children of one Father, living in unity with one another. Therefore, God's justice is realized in mankind living in *common unity*, living as the temple of God.

Those who are against justice claim that a state of injustice is the "normal" state of life, claim which is in radical opposition to the order instituted by the Creator. When Christ comes to the world, he warns us of them: *"See that you not be deceived, for many will come in my name, saying, 'I am he,' and 'The time has come.' Do not follow them!"* (*Luke* 21:8).

Unlike the true Temple, the false temple will come to an end

Using a symbolic language, Jesus describes what will happen to those nations promoting injustice – promoting the false temple –: there will be *"wars and insurrections... Nation will rise against nation, and kingdom against kingdom. There will be powerful earthquakes, famines and plagues from place to place; and awesome sights and mighty signs will come from the sky"* (*Luke* 21:9-11).

As to the *"wars and insurrections,"* human history shows they are the events that bring an end to unjust and repressive nations.

As to the *"earthquakes, famines and plagues,"* they are destructive only when injustice rules over mankind. For, wherever there is justice, people do come to the assistance of the victims of the events of nature, thus preventing or ameliorating the destructive effects of earthquakes, famines and plagues.

As to the *"awesome sights and mighty signs [coming] from the sky,"* this language emphasizes the fact that the defeat of injustice and subsequent restoration of justice are, in themselves, awesome sights and mighty signs. For those who restore justice *"there will arise the sun of justice with its healing rays"* (*Malachi* 3:20).

EPILOGUE

There are many more wondrous deeds the human community stores in its bosom. There are still many works the God incarnate yearns to do through people who promote peace, unity and justice; through people who see God in their fellow human beings, especially, in those whom God calls *my beloved "little brothers"* (*Matthew* 25:40). There are still many gifts the trinitarian God has for us so that, by receiving them, we may enrich our communitarian way of life, and, someday, live in a world where people from every segment of society may be capable of setting aside their selfish interests for the purpose of attaining the common good.

How wonderful would it be to live in a community where love of neighbor is the same as love of God! *"For I was hungry and you gave me food. I was thirsty and you gave me drink, a stranger and you welcome me, naked and you clothed me, ill and you cared for me, in prison and you visited me"* (*Matthew* 25:35-36).

How wonderful would it be to live in a community where human justice is not limited only to reward those who do good, but also to redeem those who are indifferent to the needs of their fellow humans, those who promote injustice among the members of the human race, those who foment the exploitation of man by man.

How wonderful would it be for men to allow God to get close to them, and thus, realize, once and for all, that they have the power to eradicate their greed of material wealth, which divides them into antagonistic groups. The time will come for us to embrace the God who opens his arms so that we may participate in the fraternal embrace within the universal human community.

END

Printed in the United States
by Baker & Taylor Publisher Services